THINK *and*
GROW RICH
EVERY DAY

TITLES BY NAPOLEON HILL

PUBLISHED BY TARCHER/PENGUIN

The Law of Success

Think and Grow Rich

Your Magic Power to Be Rich!

The Think and Grow Rich Workbook

The Magic Ladder to Success

The Master-Key to Riches

The Prosperity Bible

Think and Grow Rich Every Day

The Think and Grow Rich Success Journal

JEREMY P. TARCHER/PENGUIN

a member of Penguin Group (USA) Inc.

New York

THINK *and* GROW RICH EVERY DAY

· *365 Days of Success* ·

From the Inspirational Writings of

NAPOLEON HILL

with

JOEL FOTINOS & AUGUST GOLD

JEREMY P. TARCHER/PENGUIN
Published by the Penguin Group
Penguin Group (USA) Inc., 375 Hudson Street, New York, New York 10014,
USA * Penguin Group (Canada), 90 Eglinton Avenue East, Suite 700, Toronto, Ontario
M4P 2Y3, Canada (a division of Pearson Penguin Canada Inc.) * Penguin Books Ltd,
80 Strand, London WC2R 0RL, England * Penguin Ireland, 25 St Stephen's Green,
Dublin 2, Ireland (a division of Penguin Books Ltd) * Penguin Group (Australia),
250 Camberwell Road, Camberwell, Victoria 3124, Australia * (a division of Pearson
Australia Group Pty Ltd) * Penguin Books India Pvt Ltd, 11 Community Centre,
Panchsheel Park, New Delhi–110 017, India * Penguin Group (NZ), 67 Apollo Drive,
Rosedale, North Shore 0632, New Zealand (a division of Pearson
New Zealand Ltd) * Penguin Books (South Africa) (Pty) Ltd, 24 Sturdee Avenue,
Rosebank, Johannesburg 2196, South Africa

Penguin Books Ltd, Registered Offices: 80 Strand, London WC2R 0RL, England

Think and Grow Rich was first published in 1937.
The Law of Success was first published in 1928.

Most Tarcher/Penguin books are available at special quantity discounts for bulk purchase
for sales promotions, premiums, fund-raising, and educational needs. Special books or
book excerpts also can be created to fit specific needs. For details, write
Penguin Group (USA) Inc. Special Markets, 375 Hudson Street,
New York, NY 10014.

Library of Congress Cataloging-in-Publication Data

Hill, Napoleon, 1883–1970.
[Think and grow rich]
Think and grow rich every day : 365 days of success / from the inspiration writings of Napoleon Hill
with Joel Fotinos & August Gold.
p.   cm.
ISBN 978-1-58542-811-3
1. Success in business.   2. Carnegie, Andrew, 1835–1919.   I. Fotinos, Joel.   II. Gold,
August, date.   III. Title.
HF5386.H57   2010   2010025894
650.1—dc22

Printed in the United States of America
1   3   5   7   9   10   8   6   4   2

BOOK DESIGN BY AMANDA DEWEY

This publication is designed to provide accurate and authoritative information in regard to the subject
matter covered. It is sold with the understanding that neither the publisher nor the authors are engaged
in rendering legal, accounting, or other professional services. If you require legal advice or other expert
assistance, you should seek the services of a competent professional.

While the authors have made every effort to provide accurate telephone numbers and Internet addresses
at the time of publication, neither the publisher nor the authors assume any responsibility for errors, or
for changes that occur after publication. Further, the publisher does not have any control over and does
not assume any responsibility for author or third-party websites or their content.

CONTENTS

INTRODUCTION

When I first began reading *Think and Grow Rich* and applying its principles in earnest, I discovered something simple and profound. I discovered that when I read *Think and Grow Rich* every day, and in turn applied what I had read every day to my life, I experienced more success. When I didn't do those things every day, I experienced less success. This may not seem like news to anyone else, but this simple fact changed my life completely.

Up until that realization, I had read portions of the book, tried out a few of the suggestions that Napoleon Hill mentioned in the text, and even went as far as creating my "Statement of Desire," though I didn't feel the need to read it twice each day, as he instructs. I was more sporadic in my gestures, and the lack of results showed my lack of commitment. As the saying goes, half measures avail us nothing—and that certainly was my experience. At that time, I was someone who believed in "wishing and hoping" for success, without putting in the required effort to contribute to it.

But as Napoleon Hill teaches over and over, "You can't get something for nothing." So I decided to commit fully to the principles found in *Think and Grow Rich* and see where they took me.

When I committed myself to reading the book every day and doing everything that was suggested in the spirit with which Napoleon Hill wrote the book, everything began to change for me. I began to experience success almost immediately. Why? Because as Napoleon Hill suggests in his groundbreaking book *Think and Grow Rich*, when we are active in our lives each and every day, we become *engaged* in our lives. When we are engaged, we can choose to affect our lives each day, and in doing so we automatically affect every day that follows. Those who are not engaged daily in their own lives do not have that same experience.

In the years since I first discovered the joy of *Think and Grow Rich*, I have read the book many times and worked with Master Mind groups and Master Mind partners as well as taught the principles to hundreds of people in *Think and Grow Rich* workshops. I also delighted in Napoleon Hill's other magnum opus, *The Law of Success*, which contains many of the same ideas, as well as other concepts that are congruent with *Think and Grow Rich*. Out of all of this experience that my Master Mind partner, August Gold, and I have had with the principles came two projects. The first, *The Think and Grow Rich Workbook*, a companion to the original *Think and Grow Rich*, contains exercises that help readers begin to apply the suggestions of *Think and Grow Rich* to their own lives. And now comes *Think and Grow Rich Every Day*, which is a way to take the inspiration from *Think and Grow Rich* and *The Law of Success* and reap from these treasures daily.

A few notes about *Think and Grow Rich Every Day* before you begin reading. First, all the material in *Think and Grow Rich Every Day* comes from the original and public domain editions of *Think and Grow Rich* (1937) and *The Law of Success* (1928). We have, however, made very slight punctuation and other grammatical alterations and condensations so that the text will make more sense when read in daily inspirational portions. Napoleon Hill wrote this material nearly a century ago, both during and after the Great Depression, and the language of that era—

including the use of masculine pronouns and examples—
is somewhat different from that of today. We've left most
of this untouched, including occasional antiquated references or word choices, or the use of capital letters or ital-
ics to emphasize certain words or phrases, with just a few
minor adjustments for clarity.

One powerful way to read through this material is to
pick one major principle and study it for an entire month.
However, there are thirteen principles in *Think and Grow
Rich* and only twelve months in the year. We decided to
combine two of the shorter chapters of *Think and Grow
Rich*—"The Subconscious Mind" and "The Brain"—
into one month of study. In addition, since the material
is so important, we've added sections of "How to Outwit
the Six Ghosts of Fear" to the December principle of the
Sixth Sense. *Think and Grow Rich Every Day* is meant to
compliment the original texts, not replace them. If you
find yourself interested in any particular idea or principle
in *Think and Grow Rich Every Day*, we encourage you to
go to *Think and Grow Rich* and *The Law of Success* for more
exploration of Napoleon Hill's philosophy and to see the
text in its original form.

In *Think and Grow Rich*, Napoleon Hill asks readers
to take "six practical steps" that will transmute desires into

riches. These steps are key to *Think and Grow Rich*, and so we've put them at the beginning of this daily guide in the section we've titled "Your Six Steps to Success." Read through the six steps, do what they suggest, and then create your "Statement of Desire" (see page 11). Once you've set down your goal and intentions in writing, the daily readings will help you reach your goal.

Think and Grow Rich has sold millions of copies and has remained in print and on bestseller lists since its original publication in 1937. Why? Because the philosophy it contains has worked for so many people. Now it is time for you to be inspired daily!

—*Joel Fotinos and August Gold*

Your Six Steps to Success

from *Think and Grow Rich*
by Napoleon Hill

The method by which desire for riches can be transmuted into its financial equivalent consists of six definite, practical steps:

FIRST. Fix in your mind the exact amount of money you desire. It is not sufficient merely to say, "I want plenty of money." Be definite as to the amount.

SECOND. Determine exactly what you intend to give in return for the money you desire. (There is no such reality as "something for nothing.")

THIRD. Establish a definite date when you intend to *possess* the money you desire.

FOURTH. Create a definite plan for carrying out your desire, and begin *at once,* whether you are ready or not, to put this plan into *action*.

FIFTH. Write out a clear, concise statement of the amount of money you intend to acquire, name the time limit for its acquisition, state what you intend to give in return for the money, and describe clearly the plan through which you intend to accumulate it.

SIXTH. Read your written statement aloud, twice daily, once just before retiring at night, and once after arising in the morning. As you read—see and feel and believe yourself already in possession of the money.

The instructions given in connection with the six steps will now be summarized, and blended with the principles as follows:

1. Go into some quiet spot (preferably in bed at night) where you will not be disturbed or interrupted, close your eyes, and repeat

aloud (so you may hear your own words) the written statement of the amount of money you intend to accumulate, the time limit for its accumulation, and a description of the service or merchandise you intend to give in return for the money. As you carry out these instructions, see yourself already in possession of the money.

For example: Suppose that you intend to accumulate $50,000 by the first of January, five years hence, and that you intend to give personal services in return for the money, in the capacity of a salesman. Your written statement of your purpose should be similar to the following:

By the first day of January 20XX, I will have in my possession $50,000, which will come to me in various amounts from time to time during the interim.

In return for this money I will give the most efficient service of which I am capable, rendering the fullest possible quantity and the best possible quality of service in the capacity of salesman of . . .

(describe the service or merchandise you intend to sell). "I believe that I will have this money in my possession. My faith is so strong that I can now see this money before my eyes. I can touch it with my hands. It is now awaiting transfer to me at the time and in the proportion that I deliver the service I intend to render in return for it. I am awaiting a plan by which to accumulate this money, and I will follow that plan when it is received.

2. Repeat the first step night and morning until you can see (in your imagination) the money you intend to accumulate.
3. Place a written copy of your statement where you can see it night and morning, and read it just before retiring and upon arising until it has been memorized.

Remember, as you carry out these instructions, that you are applying the principle of auto-suggestion for the purpose of giving orders to your subconscious mind. Remember, also, that your subconscious mind will act only upon instructions which are emotionalized and handed over to it with "feeling." Faith is the strongest and most productive of the emotions. Follow the instructions on faith.

These instructions may, at first, seem abstract. Do not let this disturb you. Follow the instructions, no matter how abstract or impractical they may, at first, appear to be. The time will soon come, if you do as you have been instructed, *in spirit as well as in act,* when a whole new universe of power will unfold to you.

MY STATEMENT OF DESIRE

The exact amount of money I desire is:

_____

I intend to give _____
_____ in return for
the money I desire.

The definite date I intend to possess this
money by _____

_____

My definite plan of action is:
1. _____
2. _____
3. _____

Signed: _____
Date: _____

JANUARY

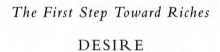

The First Step Toward Riches

DESIRE

January 1

An intangible impulse of thought can be transmuted into its physical counterpart by the application of known principles. Truly, "thoughts are things," and powerful things at that, when they are mixed with definiteness of purpose, persistence, and a burning desire for their translation into riches, or other material objects.

January 2

Every human being who reaches the age of under-standing of the purpose of money wishes for it. *Wishing* will not bring riches. But *desiring* riches with a state of mind that becomes an obsession, then planning definite ways and means to acquire riches, and backing those plans with persistence which *does not recognize failure,* will bring riches.

January 3

Every person who wins in any undertaking must be willing to burn his ships and cut all sources of retreat. Only by so doing can one be sure of maintaining that state of mind known as a burning desire to win, essential to success.

January 4

When opportunity comes, it often appears in a different form, and from a different direction than one expects. That is one of the tricks of opportunity. It has a sly habit of slipping in by the back door, and often it comes disguised in the form of misfortune, or temporary defeat. Perhaps this is why so many fail to recognize opportunity.

January 5

You may complain that it is impossible for you to "see yourself in possession of money" before you actually have it. Here is where a burning desire will come to your aid. If you truly desire money so keenly that your desire is an obsession, you will have no difficulty in convincing yourself that you will acquire it.

January 6

To the uninitiated, who has not been schooled in the working principles of the human mind, these instructions may appear impractical. It may be helpful to know that the information they convey was received from Andrew Carnegie, who began as an ordinary laborer in the steel mills but managed, despite his humble beginning, to make these principles yield him a fortune of considerably more than one hundred million. It may be of further help to know that the six steps here recommended were carefully scrutinized by the late Thomas A. Edison, who placed his stamp of approval upon them as being the steps essential for the accumulation of money, but necessary for the attainment of *any definite goal*.

January 7

We who are in this race for riches should be encouraged to know that this changed world in which we live is demanding new ideas, new ways of doing things, new leaders, new inventions, new methods of teaching, new methods of marketing, new books, new literature, new features for the radio, new ideas for moving pictures. Back of all this demand for new and better things, there is one quality which one must possess to win, and that is definiteness of purpose, the knowledge of what one wants, and a burning desire to possess it. This changed world requires practical dreamers who can *and will* put their dreams into action. The practical dreamers have always been and always will be the pattern makers of civilization.

January 8

When you begin to think and grow rich, you will observe that riches begin with a state of mind, with definiteness of purpose, with little or no hard work. You, and every other person, ought to be interested in knowing how to acquire that state of mind which will attract riches. I spent twenty-five years in research, analyzing more than 25,000 people, because I, too, wanted to know "how wealthy men become that way."

January 9

Life is strange and often imponderable! Both the successes and the failures have their roots in simple experiences. Yet to prosper by these experiences, you must *analyze them* and find the lesson within. One sound idea is all that one needs to achieve success.

January 10

When riches begin to come, they come so quickly, in such great abundance, that one wonders where they have been hiding during all those lean years. This is an astounding statement, and all the more so when we take into consideration the popular belief that riches come only to those who work hard and long.

January 11

When Henley wrote the prophetic lines "I am the Master of my Fate, I am the Captain of my Soul," he should have informed us that we are the Masters of our Fate, the Captains of our Souls, *because* we have the power to control our thoughts. He should have told us that the ether in which this little earth floats, in which we move and have our being, is a form of energy moving at an inconceivably high rate of vibration, and that the ether is filled with a form of universal power which adapts itself to the nature of the thoughts we hold in our minds and influences us, in natural ways, to transmute our thoughts into their physical equivalent.

January 12

The world has become accustomed to new discoveries. Nay, it has shown a willingness to reward the dreamer who gives the world a new idea. "The greatest achievement was, at first, and for a time, but a dream." "The oak sleeps in the acorn. The bird waits in the egg, and in the highest vision of the soul, a waking angel stirs. Dreams are the seedlings of reality."

January 13

To succeed you must choose a definite desire; place all your energy, all your willpower, all your effort, everything back of that goal. Stand by your desire until it becomes the dominating obsession of your life—and, finally, a fact.

January 14

Success comes to those who become success conscious. Failure comes to those who indifferently allow themselves to become failure conscious. The object is to learn the art of changing your mind from failure consciousness to success consciousness.

January 15

We refuse to believe that which we do not understand. We foolishly believe that our own limitations are the proper measure of limitations. Millions of people look at the achievements of Henry Ford and envy him, because of his good fortune, or luck, or genius, or whatever it is that they credit for Ford's fortune. Perhaps one person in every hundred thousand knows the secret of Ford's success, and those who do know are too modest, or too reluctant, to speak of it, *because of its simplicity*. Henry Ford was a success, because he understood and *applied* the principles of success. One of these is desire: knowing what one wants.

January 16

The object is to want money and to become so determined to have it that you convince yourself you will have it. Only those who become "money conscious" ever accumulate great riches. "Money consciousness" means that the mind has become so thoroughly saturated with the desire for money that one can see one's self already in possession of it.

January 17

Our mind makes no attempt to discriminate between destructive thoughts and constructive thoughts; it will urge us to translate into physical reality thoughts of poverty just as quickly as it will influence us to act upon thoughts of riches. Our brains become magnetized with the dominating thoughts which we hold in our minds, and, by means with which no man is familiar, these "magnets" attract to us the forces, the people, the circumstances of life which harmonize with the nature of our *dominating* thoughts.

January 18

Before we can accumulate riches in great abundance, we must magnetize our minds with an intense desire for riches; we must become "money conscious" until the desire for money drives us to create definite plans for acquiring it.

January 19

We who desire to accumulate riches should remember the real leaders of the world always have been men who harnessed, and put into practical use, the intangible, unseen forces of unborn opportunity, and have converted those forces (or impulses of thought), into skyscrapers, cities, factories, airplanes, automobiles, and every form of convenience that makes life more pleasant.

Tolerance and an open mind are practical necessities of the dreamer of today. Those who are afraid of new ideas are doomed before they start. Never has there been a time more favorable to pioneers than the present. True, there is no wild and woolly West to be conquered, as in the days of the covered wagon, but there is a vast business, financial, and industrial world to be remolded and redirected along new and better lines.

January 20

In planning to acquire your share of the riches, let no one influence you to scorn the dreamer. To win the big stakes in this changed world, you must catch the spirit of the great pioneers of the past, whose dreams have given to civilization all that it has of value, the spirit which serves as the lifeblood of our own country—your opportunity, and mine, to develop and market our talents.

Let us not forget, Columbus dreamed of an unknown world, staked his life on the existence of such a world, and discovered it!

Copernicus, the great astronomer, dreamed of a multiplicity of worlds, and revealed them! No one denounced him as "impractical" *after* he had triumphed. Instead, the world worshipped at his shrine, thus proving once more that "success requires no apologies, failure permits no alibis."

January 21

If the thing you wish to do is right and *you believe in it,* go ahead and do it! Put your dream across, and never mind what "they" say if you meet with temporary defeat, for "they," perhaps, do not know that every failure brings with it the seed of an equivalent success.

January 22

I believe in the power of desire backed by faith, because I have seen this power lift men from lowly beginnings to places of power and wealth; I have seen it rob the grave of its victims; I have seen it serve as the medium by which men staged a comeback after having been defeated in a hundred different ways; I have seen it provide my own son with a normal, happy, successful life, despite Nature's having sent him into the world without ears.

Through some strange and powerful principle of "mental chemistry" which she has never divulged, Nature wraps up in the impulse of strong desire "that something" which recognizes no such word as *impossible*, and accepts no such reality as failure.

January 23

It is my duty, and a privilege to say I believe, and not without reason, that nothing is impossible to the person who backs desire with enduring faith.

Verily, a burning desire has devious ways of transmuting itself into its physical equivalent.

Strange and imponderable is the power of the human mind! We do not understand the method by which it uses every circumstance, every individual, every physical thing within its reach, as a means of transmuting desire into its physical counterpart. Perhaps science will uncover this secret.

January 24

Truly, my own son has taught me that handicaps can be converted into stepping-stones on which one may climb toward some worthy goal, unless they are accepted as obstacles and used as alibis.

Think of the words of the immortal Emerson: "The whole course of things goes to teach us faith. We need only obey. There is guidance for each of us, and by lowly listening, we shall hear *the right word*." The right word? *Desire!*

January 25

Kindle anew in your mind the fire of hope, faith, courage, and tolerance. If you have these states of mind and a working knowledge of the principles described, all else that you need will come to you when you are ready for it. Let Emerson state the thought in these words: "Every proverb, every book, every byword that belongs to thee for aid and comfort shall surely come home through open or winding passages. Every friend whom not thy fantastic will, but the great and tender soul in thee craveth, shall lock thee in his embrace."

There is a difference between wishing for a thing and being ready to receive it. No one is *ready* for a thing until he *believes* he can acquire it. The state of mind must be belief, not mere hope or wish. Open-mindedness is essential for belief. Closed minds do not inspire faith, courage, and belief.

Remember, no more effort is required to aim high in life, to demand abundance and prosperity, than is required to accept misery and poverty.

January 27

Awake, arise, and assert yourself, you dreamers of the world. Your star is now in the ascendency. The world depression brought the opportunity you have been waiting for. It taught people humility, tolerance, and open-mindedness.

The world is filled with an abundance of opportunity which the dreamers of the past never knew. A burning desire to be and to do is the starting point from which the dreamer must take off. Dreams are not born of indifference, laziness, or lack of ambition. The world no longer scoffs at the dreamer, nor calls him impractical.

January 28

You have been disappointed, you have undergone defeat during the depression, you have felt the great heart within you crushed until it bled. Take courage, for these experiences have tempered the spiritual metal of which you are made—they are assets of incomparable value.

January 29

Remember that all who succeed in life get off to a bad start and pass through many heartbreaking struggles before they "arrive." The turning point in the lives of those who succeed usually comes at the moment of some crisis, through which they are introduced to their "other selves."

O. Henry discovered the genius which slept within his brain after he had met with great misfortune and was confined in a prison cell. Being forced, through misfortune, to become acquainted with his "other self" and to use his imagination, he discovered himself to be a great author instead of a miserable criminal and outcast.

January 30

Life is strange, and often imponderable! Both the successes and the failures have their roots in simple experiences. Yet to prosper by these experiences, you must *analyze them* and find the lesson within.

January 31

It is most appalling to know that ninety-five per cent of the people of the world are drifting aimlessly through life, without the slightest conception of the work for which they are best fitted and with no conception whatsoever of even the need of such a thing as a definite objective toward which to strive.

There is a psychological as well as an economic reason for the selection of a definite chief aim in life. It is a well-established principle of psychology that a person's acts are always in harmony with the dominating thoughts of his or her mind.

Any definite chief aim that is deliberately fixed in the mind and held there, with the determination to realize it, finally saturates the entire subconscious mind until it automatically influences the physical action of the body toward the attainment of that purpose.

FEBRUARY

 The Second Step Toward Riches

FAITH

February 1

Faith is the head chemist of the mind. When faith is blended with the vibration of thought, the subconscious mind instantly picks up the vibration, translates it into its spiritual equivalent, and transmits it to Infinite Intelligence, as in the case of prayer.

February 2

One of the greatest powers for good, upon the face of this earth, is faith. To this marvelous power may be traced miracles of the most astounding nature. If offers peace on earth to all who embrace it.

Faith involves a principle that is so far-reaching in its effect that no man can say what are its limitations, or if it has limitations.

February 3

The emotions of faith, love, and sex are the most powerful of all the major positive emotions. When the three are blended, they have the effect of "coloring" the vibration of thought in such a way that it instantly reaches the subconscious mind, where it is changed into its spiritual equivalent, the only form that induces a response from Infinite Intelligence.

February 4

Love and faith are psychic, related to the spiritual side of man. Sex is purely biological, and related only to the physical. The mixing, or blending, of these three emotions has the effect of opening a direct line of communication between the finite, thinking mind of man and Infinite Intelligence.

February 5

Faith is a state of mind which may be induced, or created, by affirmation or repeated instructions to the subconscious mind, through the principle of auto-suggestion. Repetition of affirmation of orders to your subconscious mind is the only known method of voluntary development of the emotion of faith. This is the equivalent of saying that any impulse of thought which is repeatedly passed on to the subconscious mind is, finally, accepted and acted upon by the subconscious mind, which proceeds to translate that impulse into its physical equivalent, by the most practical procedure available.

February 6

Consider again the statement, all thoughts which have been emotionalized (given feeling) and mixed with faith begin immediately to translate themselves into their physical equivalent or counterpart. The emotions, or the "feeling" portion of thoughts, are the factors which give thoughts vitality, life, and action. The emotions of faith, love, and sex, when mixed with any thought impulse, give it greater action than any of these emotions can do singly.

Not only thought impulses which have been mixed with faith but those which have been mixed with any of the positive emotions or any of the negative emotions may reach and influence the subconscious mind.

February 7

The subconscious mind will translate into its physical equivalent a thought impulse of a negative or destructive nature just as readily as it will act upon thought impulses of a positive or constructive nature. This accounts for the strange phenomenon which so many millions of people experience, referred to as "misfortune" or "bad luck."

There are millions of people who believe themselves "doomed" to poverty and failure, because of some strange force over which they believe they have no control. They are the creators of their own "misfortunes," because of this negative belief, which is picked up by the subconscious mind and translated into its physical equivalent.

February 8

You may benefit by passing on to your subconscious mind any desire which you wish translated into its physical or monetary equivalent in a state of expectancy or belief that the transmutation will actually take place. Your belief, or faith, is the element which determines the action of your subconscious mind. There is nothing to hinder you from "deceiving" your subconscious mind when giving it instructions through auto-suggestion.

To make this "deceit" more realistic, conduct yourself just as you would if you were already in possession of the material thing which you are demanding when you call upon your subconscious mind.

The subconscious mind will transmute into its physical equivalent, by the most direct and practical media available, any order which is given to it in a state of belief or faith that the order will be carried out.

February 9

If it be true that one may become a criminal by association with crime (and this is a known fact), it is equally true that one may develop faith by voluntarily suggesting to the subconscious mind that one has faith. The mind comes, finally, to take on the nature of the influences which dominate it. Understand this truth, and you will know why it is essential for you to encourage the *positive emotions* as dominating forces of your mind and discourage—and *eliminate*—negative emotions.

February 10

A mind dominated by positive emotions becomes a favorable abode for the state of mind known as faith. A mind so dominated may, at will, give the subconscious mind instructions, which it will accept and act upon immediately.

February 11

Faith is a state of mind which may be induced by auto-suggestion. Faith may be developed where it does not already exist.

Have faith in yourself; faith in the Infinite.

February 12

It is a well known fact that one comes, finally, to believe whatever one repeats to one's self, *whether the statement be true or false.* If a man repeats a lie over and over, he will eventually accept the lie as truth. Moreover, he will believe it to be the truth. Every man is what he is because of the dominating thoughts which he permits to occupy his mind. The thoughts which a man deliberately places in his own mind, and encourages with sympathy, and with which he mixes any one or more of the emotions, constitute the motivating forces which direct and control his every movement, act, and deed!

February 13

Thoughts which are mixed with any of the feelings of emotions constitute a "magnetic" force which attracts, from the vibrations of the ether, other similar or related thoughts. A thought thus "magnetized" with emotion may be compared to a seed which, when planted in fertile soil, germinates, grows, and multiplies itself over and over again, until that which was originally one small seed becomes countless millions of seeds of the same brand!

February 14

The ether is a great cosmic mass of eternal forces of vibration. It is made up of both destructive vibrations and constructive vibrations. It carries, at all times, vibrations of fear, poverty, disease, failure, misery; and vibrations of prosperity, health, success, and happiness.

From the great storehouse of the ether, the human mind is constantly attracting vibrations which harmonize with that which dominates the human mind. Any thought, idea, plan, or purpose which one *holds* in one's mind attracts, from the vibrations of the ether, a host of its relatives, adds these "relatives" to its own force, and grows until it becomes the dominating, motivating master of the individual in whose mind it has been housed.

February 15

Now, let us go back to the starting point and become informed as to how the original seed of an idea, plan, or purpose may be planted in the mind. The information is easily conveyed: Any idea, plan, or purpose may be placed in the mind *through repetition of thought*. This is why you are asked to write out a statement of your major purpose, or Definite Chief Aim, commit it to memory, and repeat it, in audible words, day after day, until these vibrations of sound have reached your subconscious mind.

We are what we are because of the vibrations of thought which we pick up and register through the stimuli of our daily environment.

February 16

Resolve to throw off the influences of any unfortunate environment and to build your own life to order. Taking inventory of mental assets and liabilities, you will discover that your greatest weakness is lack of self-confidence. This handicap can be surmounted, and timidity translated into courage, through the aid of the principle of auto-suggestion. The application of this principle may be made through a simple arrangement of positive thought impulses stated in writing, memorized, and repeated, until they become a part of the working equipment of the subconscious faculty of your mind.

February 17

SELF-CONFIDENCE FORMULA #1
(Memorize and repeat daily.)

I know that I have the ability to achieve the object of my Definite Purpose in life; therefore, I demand of myself persistent, continuous action toward its attainment, and I here and now promise to render such action.

February 18

SELF-CONFIDENCE FORMULA #2
(Memorize and repeat daily.)

I realize the dominating thoughts of my mind will eventually reproduce themselves in outward, physical action and gradually transform themselves into physical reality; therefore, I will concentrate my thoughts for thirty minutes daily upon the task of thinking of the person I intend to become, thereby creating in my mind a clear mental picture of that person.

February 19

SELF-CONFIDENCE FORMULA #3
(Memorize and repeat daily.)

I know through the principle of auto-suggestion any desire that I persistently hold in my mind will eventually seek expression through some practical means of attaining the object back of it; therefore I will devote ten minutes daily to demanding of myself the development of self-confidence.

February 20

SELF-CONFIDENCE FORMULA #4
(Memorize and repeat daily.)

I have clearly written down a description of my Definite Chief Aim in life, and I will never stop trying until I shall have developed sufficient self-confidence for its attainment.

February 21

SELF-CONFIDENCE FORMULA #5
(Memorize and repeat daily.)

I fully realize that no wealth or position can long endure unless built upon truth and justice; therefore, I will engage in no transaction which does not benefit all whom it affects. I will succeed by attracting to myself the forces I wish to use and the cooperation of other people. I will induce others to serve me, because of my willingness to serve others. I will eliminate hatred, envy, jealousy, selfishness, and cynicism by developing love for all humanity, because I know that a negative attitude toward others can never bring me success. I will cause others to believe in me, because I will believe in them and in myself.

February 22

The subconscious mind (the chemical laboratory in which all thought impulses are combined and made ready for translation into physical reality) makes no distinction between constructive and destructive thought impulses. It works with the material we feed it, through our thought impulses. The subconscious mind will translate into reality a thought driven by fear just as readily as it will translate into reality a thought driven by courage, or faith.

Just as electricity will turn the wheels of industry and render useful service if used constructively, or snuff out life if wrongly used, so will the law of auto-suggestion lead you to peace and prosperity or down into the valley of misery, failure, and death, according to your degree of understanding and application of it.

February 23

If you fill your mind with fear, doubt, and unbelief in your ability to connect with and use the forces of Infinite Intelligence, the law of auto-suggestion will take this spirit of unbelief and use it as a pattern by which your subconscious mind will translate it into its physical equivalent.

The law of auto-suggestion, through which any person may rise to altitudes of achievement which stagger the imagination, is well described in the following verse:

> *If you think you are beaten, you are,*
> *If you think you dare not, you don't*
> *If you like to win, but you think you can't,*
> *It is almost certain you won't.*
> *If you think you'll lose, you're lost*
> *For out of the world we find,*
> *Success begins with a fellow's will—*
> *It's all in the state of mind.*
> *If you think you are outclassed, you are,*
> *You've got to think high to rise,*
> *You've got to be sure of yourself before*

You can ever win a prize.
Life's battles don't always go
To the stronger or faster man,
But soon or late the man who wins
Is the man who thinks he can!

February 24

You should be reminded again that:

Faith is the "eternal elixir" which gives life, power, and action to the impulse of thought!

The foregoing sentence is worth reading a second time, and a third, and a fourth. It is worth reading aloud!

Faith is the starting point of all accumulation of riches!

Faith is the basis of all "miracles," and all mysteries which cannot be analyzed by the rules of science!

Faith is the only known antidote for failure!

Faith is the element, the "chemical" which, when mixed with prayer, gives one direct communication with Infinite Intelligence.

Faith is the element which transforms the ordinary vibration of thought, created by the finite mind of man, into the spiritual equivalent.

Faith is the only agency through which the cosmic force of Infinite Intelligence can be harnessed and used by man.

February 25

Somewhere in your makeup (perhaps in the cells of your brain) there lies *sleeping* the seed of achievement, which, if aroused and put into action, would carry you to heights such as you may never have hoped to attain.

Just as a master musician may cause the most beautiful strains of music to pour forth from the strings of a violin, so may you arouse the genius which lies asleep in your brain and cause it to drive you upward to whatever goal you may wish to achieve.

Abraham Lincoln was a failure at everything he tried, until he was well past the age of forty. He was a Mr. Nobody from Nowhere until a great experience came into his life, aroused the sleeping genius within his heart and brain, and gave the world one of its really great men.

That "experience" was mixed with the emotions of sorrow and love. It came to him through Anne Rutledge, the only woman whom he ever truly loved.

February 26

It is a known fact that the emotion of love is closely akin to the state of mind known as faith, and this for the reason that love comes very near to translating one's thought impulses into their spiritual equivalent. During his work of research, the author discovered, from the analysis of the lifework and achievements of hundreds of men of outstanding accomplishment, that there was the influence of a woman's love back of nearly every one of them. The emotion of love, in the human heart and brain, creates a favorable field of magnetic attraction, which causes an influx of the higher and finer vibrations which are afloat in the ether.

February 27

The sum and substance of the teachings and the achievements of Christ, which may have been interpreted as "miracles," were nothing more or less than faith. If there are any such phenomena as "miracles" they are produced only through the state of mind known as faith!

Let us consider the power of faith as demonstrated by Mahatma Gandhi. In this man the world had one of the most astounding examples known to civilization of the possibilities of faith. Gandhi wielded more potential power than any man of his time, despite the fact that he had none of the orthodox tools of power, such as money, battleships, soldiers, and materials of warfare. Gandhi accomplished, through the influence of faith, that which the strongest military power on earth could not, and never will, accomplish through soldiers and military equipment. He accomplished the astounding feat of influencing two hundred million minds to coalesce and move in unison as a single mind. What other force on earth, except faith, could do as much?

February 28

Riches begin in the form of thought!

The amount is limited only by the person in whose mind the thought is put into motion. Faith removes limitations! Remember this when you are ready to bargain with Life for whatever it is that you ask as your price for having passed this way.

Remember, also, that the man who created the United States Steel Corporation was practically unknown at the time. He was merely Andrew Carnegie's "Man Friday" until he gave birth to his famous IDEA. After that he quickly rose to a position of power, fame, and riches.

There are no limitations to the mind except those we *acknowledge*.

Both *poverty* and *riches* are the offspring of thought.

MARCH

The Third Step Toward Riches

AUTO-SUGGESTION

March 1

Auto-suggestion is a term which applies to all suggestions and all self-administered stimuli which reach one's mind through the five senses. Stated in another way, auto-suggestion is self-suggestion. It is the agency of communication between that part of the mind where conscious thought takes place and that which serves as the seat of action for the subconscious mind.

Through the dominating thoughts which one *permits* to remain in the conscious mind (whether these thoughts be negative or positive, is immaterial), the principle of auto-suggestion voluntarily reaches the subconscious mind and influences it with these thoughts.

March 2

No thought, whether it be negative or positive, can enter the subconscious mind without the aid of the principle of auto-suggestion, with the exception of thoughts picked up from the ether.

Stated differently, all sense impressions which are perceived through the five senses are stopped by the conscious thinking mind and may be either passed on to the subconscious mind, or rejected, at will. The conscious faculty serves, therefore, as an outer-guard to the approach of the subconscious.

March 3

Nature has so built man that he has absolute control over the material which reaches his subconscious mind through his five senses, although this is not meant to be construed as a statement that man always exercises this control. In the great majority of instances, he does not exercise it, which explains why so many people go through life in poverty.

March 4

The subconscious mind resembles a fertile garden spot in which weeds will grow in abundance if the seeds of more desirable crops are not sown therein. Auto-suggestion is the agency of control through which an individual may voluntarily feed his subconscious mind on thoughts of a creative nature or, by neglect, permit thoughts of a destructive nature to find their way into this rich garden of the mind.

March 5

You were instructed earlier to read aloud twice daily the written statement of your desire for money and to see and feel yourself already in possession of the money! By following these instructions, you communicate the object of your desire directly to your subconscious mind in a spirit of absolute faith. Through repetition of this procedure, you voluntarily create thought habits which are favorable to your efforts to transmute desire into its monetary equivalent.

March 6

When reading aloud the statement of your desire (through which you are endeavoring to develop a "money consciousness"), the mere reading of the words is of no consequence—unless you mix emotion, or feeling, with your words. Your subconscious mind recognizes and acts upon only thoughts which have been well mixed with emotion or feeling. This is the main reason the majority of people who try to apply the principle of auto-suggestion get no desirable results. Plain, unemotional words do not influence the subconscious mind. You will get no appreciable results until you learn to reach your subconscious mind with thoughts or spoken words which have been well emotionalized with belief.

March 7

Do not become discouraged if you cannot control and direct your emotions the first time you try to do so. Remember, there is no such possibility as something for nothing. Ability to reach and influence your subconscious mind has its price, and you must pay that price. You cannot cheat, even if you desire to do so. The price of ability to influence your subconscious mind is everlasting persistence in applying the principles described here. You cannot develop the desired ability for a lower price. You, and you alone, must decide whether or not the reward for which you are striving (the "money consciousness") is worth the price you must pay for it in effort.

March 8

Wisdom and "cleverness" alone will not attract and retain money except in a few very rare instances, where the law of averages favors the attraction of money through these sources. The method of attracting money described here does not depend upon the law of averages. Moreover, the method plays no favorites. It will work for one person as effectively as it will for another. Where failure is experienced, it is the individual, *not the method,* which has failed. If you try and fail, make another effort, and still another, until you succeed.

March 9

It will be necessary for you to make sure of the principle of concentration. When you begin to carry out the first of the six steps, which instructs you to "fix in your own mind the exact amount of money you desire," hold your thoughts on that amount of money by concentration, or fixation or attention, with your eyes closed, until you can actually see the physical appearance of the money. Do this at least once each day.

March 10

Your ability to use the principle of auto-suggestion will depend very largely upon your capacity to concentrate upon a given desire until that desire becomes a burning obsession.

When you begin to carry out the first of the six steps, which instructs you to "fix in your own mind the exact amount of money you desire," hold your thoughts on that amount of money by concentration, or fixation of attention, with your eyes closed, until you can actually see the physical appearance of the money. Do this at least once each day. As you go through these exercises, follow the instructions given in the chapter on faith, and see yourself actually in possession of the money!

March 11

Here is a most significant fact: The subconscious mind takes any orders given it in a spirit of absolute faith and acts upon those orders, although the orders often have to be presented *over and over again,* through repetition, before they are interpreted by the subconscious mind. Following the preceding statement, consider the possibility of playing a perfectly legitimate "trick" on your subconscious mind, by making it believe, *because you believe it,* that you must have the amount of money you are visualizing, that this money is already awaiting your claim, that the subconscious mind must hand over to you practical plans for acquiring the money which is yours.

March 12

Hand over the thought suggested in the preceding day to your imagination, and see what your imagination can or will do to create practical plans for the accumulation of money through transmutation of your desire.

Begin at once to see yourself in possession of the money, demanding and expecting meanwhile that your subconscious mind will hand over the plan, or plans, you need. Be on the alert for these plans, and when they appear, put them into action immediately. When the plans appear, they will probably "flash" into your mind through the sixth sense, in the form of an "inspiration." This inspiration may be considered a direct "telegram," or message, from Infinite Intelligence. Treat it with respect, and act upon it as soon as you receive it. Failure to do this will be fatal to your success.

March 13

In the fourth of the six steps (see page 7), you were instructed to "Create a definite plan for carrying out your desire, and begin at once to put this plan into action." You should follow this instruction in the manner described in the preceding day (*March 12*). Do not trust to your "reason" when creating your plan for accumulating money through the transmutation of desire. Your reason is faulty. Moreover, your reasoning faculty may be lazy, and, if you depend entirely upon it to serve you, it may disappoint you.

When visualizing the money you intend to accumulate (with closed eyes), *see yourself rendering the service or delivering the merchandise you intend to give in return for this money. This is important!*

March 14

To get satisfactory results, you must follow all instructions in this book in a spirit of faith. If you choose to follow some of the instructions but neglect or refuse to follow others—*you will fail!*

March 15

You cannot talk initiative to others without developing a desire to practice it yourself. Through the operation of the principle of auto-suggestion every statement that you make to others leaves its imprint on your own subconscious mind, and this holds good whether your statements are false or true.

You have often heard the saying "He who lives by the sword will die by the sword."

Properly interpreted, this simply means that we are constantly attracting to ourselves and weaving into our own characters and personalities those qualities which our influence is helping to create in others. If we help others develop the habit of initiative, we, in turn, develop this same habit. If we sow the seeds of hatred and envy and discouragement in others, we, in turn, develop these qualities in ourselves.

March 16

When your own mind is vibrating at a high rate, because it has been stimulated with enthusiasm, that vibration registers in the minds of all within its radius, and especially in the minds of those with whom you come in close contact. When a public speaker "senses" the feeling that his audience is "en rapport" (in harmony) with him he merely recognizes the fact that his own enthusiasm has influenced the minds of his listeners until their minds are vibrating in harmony with his own.

When the salesman "senses" the fact that the "psychological" moment for closing a sale has arrived, he merely feels the effect of his own enthusiasm as it influences the mind of his prospective buyer and places that mind "en rapport" with his own.

March 17

Skepticism, in connection with all new ideas, is characteristic of all human beings. But if you follow the instructions outlined in *Think and Grow Rich*, your skepticism will soon be replaced by belief, and this, in turn, will soon become crystallized into absolute faith. Then you will have arrived at the point where you may truly say, "I am the master of my fate, I am the captain of my soul!"

March 18

Many philosophers have made the statement that man is the master of his own *earthly* destiny, but most of them have failed to say *why* he is the master. The reason that man may become the master of himself and of his environment is because he has the power to influence his own subconscious mind, and through it gain the cooperation of Infinite Intelligence.

March 19

The actual performance of transmuting desire into money involves the use of auto-suggestion as an agency by which one may reach, and influence, the subconscious mind. The other principles are simply tools with which to apply auto-suggestion. Keep this thought in mind, and you will, at all times, be conscious of the important part the principle of auto-suggestion is to play in your efforts to accumulate money through the methods described in this book.

Carry out these instructions as though you were a small child. Inject into your efforts something of the faith of a child. The author has been most careful to see that no impractical instructions were included, because of his sincere desire to be helpful.

March 20

The vibrations of fear pass from one mind to another just as quickly and as surely as the sound of the human voice passes from the broadcasting station to the receiving set of a radio—and by the self-same medium.

Mental telepathy is a reality. Thoughts pass from one mind to another, voluntarily, whether or not this fact is recognized by either the person releasing the thoughts or the persons who pick up those thoughts.

March 21

The person who gives expression, by word of mouth, to negative or destructive thoughts is practically certain to experience the results of those words in the form of a destructive "kickback." The release of destructive thought impulses alone, without the aid of words, produces also a "kickback" in more ways than one. First of all, and perhaps most important to be remembered, the person who releases thoughts of a destructive nature must suffer damage through the breaking down of the faculty of creative imagination. Secondly, the presence in the mind of any destructive emotion develops a negative personality which repels people and often converts them into antagonists. The third source of damage to the person who entertains or releases negative thoughts lies in this significant fact—these thought-impulses are not only damaging to others, but they imbed themselves in the subconscious mind of the person releasing them and there become a part of his character.

March 22

One is never through with a thought merely by releasing it. When a thought is released, it spreads in every direction, through the medium of the ether, but it also plants itself *permanently* in the subconscious mind of *the person releasing it.*

Your business in life is presumably to achieve success. To be successful, you must find peace of mind, acquire the material needs of life, and, above all, attain happiness. All of these evidences of success begin in the form of thought impulses.

March 23

You may control your own mind; you have the power to feed it whatever thought impulses you choose. With this privilege goes also the responsibility of using it constructively. You are the master of your own earthly destiny just as surely as you have the power to control your own thoughts. You may influence, direct, and eventually control your own environment, making your life what you want it to be—or you may neglect to exercise the privilege which is yours, to make your life to order, thus casting yourself upon the broad sea of "Circumstance," where you will be tossed hither and yon, like a chip on the waves of the ocean.

March 24

The principle of psychology through which you can impress your definite chief aim upon your subconscious mind is called auto-suggestion, or suggestion which you repeatedly make to yourself. It is a degree of self-hypnotism, but do not be afraid of it on that account, for it was this same principle through the aid of which Napoleon lifted himself from the lowly station of poverty-stricken Corsican to the dictatorship of France. It was through the aid of this same principle that Thomas A. Edison has risen from the lowly beginning of a news butcher to where he is accepted as the leading inventor of the world. You need have no fear of the principle of auto-suggestion as long as you are sure that the objective for which you are striving is one that will bring you happiness of an enduring nature. Be sure that your definite purpose is constructive, that its attainment will bring hardship and misery to no one; that it will bring you peace and prosperity; then apply, to the limit of your understanding, the principle of self-suggestion for the speedy attainment of this purpose.

March 25

The subconscious mind may be likened to a magnet, and when it has been vitalized and thoroughly saturated with any definite purpose it has a decided tendency to attract all that is necessary for the fulfillment of that purpose. Like attracts like, and you may see evidence of this law in every blade of grass and every growing tree. The acorn attracts from the soil and the air the necessary materials out of which to grow an oak tree. It never grows a tree that is part oak and part poplar.

And men are subject, also, to this same Law of Attraction. Go into any cheap boardinghouse district in any city, and there you will find people of the same general trend of mind associated together. On the other hand, go into any prosperous community, and there you will find people of the same general tendencies associated together. Men who are successful always seek the company of others who are successful, while men who are on the ragged side of life always seek the company of those who are in similar circumstances. "Misery loves company."

March 26

You will attract to you people who harmonize with your own philosophy of life, whether you wish it or not. This being true, can you not see the importance of vitalizing your mind with a definite chief aim that will attract to you people who will be of help to you and not a hindrance? Suppose your definite chief aim is far above your present station in life. What of it? It is your privilege— nay, your DUTY—to aim high in life. You owe it to yourself and to the community in which you live to set a high standard for yourself.

There is much evidence to justify the belief that nothing within reason is beyond the possibility of attainment by the man whose definite chief aim has been well developed.

March 27

No undesirable environment is strong enough to hold the man or woman who understands how to apply the principle of auto-suggestion in the creation of a definite chief aim. Such a person can throw off the shackles of poverty; destroy the most deadly disease germs; rise from a lowly station in life to power and plenty.

All great leaders base their leadership upon a definite chief aim. Followers are willing followers when they know that their leader is a person with a definite chief aim who has the courage to back up that purpose with action. Even a balky horse knows when a driver with a definite chief aim takes hold of the reins and yields to that driver. When a man with a definite chief aim starts through a crowd everybody stands aside and makes a way for him, but let a man hesitate and show by his actions that he is not sure which way he wants to go, and the crowd will step all over his toes and refuse to budge an inch out of his way.

March 28

Science has established, beyond the slightest room for doubt, that through the principle of auto-suggestion any deeply rooted desire saturates the entire body and mind with the nature of the desire and literally transforms the mind into a powerful magnet that will attract the object of the desire, if it be within reason. For example, merely desiring an automobile will not cause that automobile to come rolling in, but, if there is a burning desire for an automobile, that desire will lead to the appropriate action through which an automobile may be paid for.

Merely desiring freedom would never release a man who was confined in prison if it were not sufficiently strong to cause him to do something to entitle himself to freedom.

These are the steps leading from desire to fulfillment: first the burning desire, then the crystallization of that desire into a definite purpose, then sufficient appropriate action to achieve that purpose. Remember that these three steps are always necessary to ensure success.

March 29

Not only does lack of the necessity for struggle lead to weakness of ambition and willpower, but, what is more dangerous still, it sets up in a person's mind a state of lethargy that leads to the loss of self-confidence. The person who has quit struggling because effort is no longer necessary is literally applying the principle of auto-suggestion in undermining his own power of self-confidence. Such a person will finally drift into a frame of mind in which he will actually look with more or less contempt upon the person who is forced to carry on.

The human mind, if you will pardon repetition, may be likened to an electric battery: It may be positive or it may be negative. Self-confidence is the quality with which the mind is recharged and made positive.

March 30

You learned that any idea you firmly fix in your subconscious mind by repeated affirmation automatically becomes a plan or blueprint which an unseen power uses in directing your efforts toward the attainment of the objective named in the plan.

You have also learned that the principle through which you may fix any idea you choose in your mind is called auto-suggestion, which simply means a suggestion that you give to your own mind. It was this principle of auto-suggestion that Emerson had in mind when he wrote:

"Nothing can bring you peace but yourself!"

You might well remember that *Nothing* can bring you success but yourself. Of course you will need the cooperation of others if you aim to attain success of a far-reaching nature, but you will never get that cooperation unless you vitalize your mind with the positive attitude of self-confidence.

March 31

Habit grows out of environment, out of doing the same thing or thinking the same thoughts or repeating the same words over and over again. Habit may be likened to the groove on a phonograph record, while the human mind may be likened to the needle that fits into that groove.

When any habit has been well formed, through repetition of thought or action, the mind has a tendency to attach itself to and follow the course of that habit as closely as the phonograph needle follows the groove in the wax record.

Habit is created by repeatedly directing one or more of the five senses of seeing, hearing, smelling, tasting, and feeling in a given direction.

APRIL

The Fourth Step Toward Riches

SPECIALIZED KNOWLEDGE

April 1

There are two kinds of knowledge: One is general; the other is specialized. General knowledge, no matter how great in quantity or variety it may be, is of but little use in the accumulation of money. Knowledge will not attract money, unless it is organized, and intelligently directed, through practical plans of action to the definite end of accumulation of money. Lack of understanding of this fact has been the source of confusion to millions of people who falsely believe that "knowledge is power." It is nothing of the sort! Knowledge is only *potential* power. It becomes power only when, and if, it is organized into definite plans of action and directed to a definite end.

April 2

An educated man is not necessarily one who has an abundance of general or specialized knowledge. An educated man is one who has so developed the faculties of his mind that he may acquire anything he wants, or its equivalent, without violating the rights of others.

April 3

Before you can be sure of your ability to transmute desire into its monetary equivalent, you will require specialized knowledge of the service, merchandise, or profession which you intend to offer in return for fortune. Perhaps you may need much more specialized knowledge than you have the ability or the inclination to acquire, and if this should be true, you may bridge your weakness through the aid of your Master Mind group.

April 4

Men sometimes go through life suffering from inferiority complexes because they are not men of "education." The man who can organize and direct a Master Mind group of men who possess knowledge useful in the accumulation of money is just as much a man of education as any man in the group. Remember this if you suffer from a feeling of inferiority because your schooling has been limited.

April 5

Specialized knowledge is among the most plentiful, and the cheapest, forms of service which may be had!

First of all, decide the sort of specialized knowledge you require and the purpose for which it is needed. To a large extent your major purpose in life, the goal toward which you are working, will help determine what knowledge you need. With this question settled, your next move requires that you have accurate information concerning dependable sources of knowledge. The more important of these are:

a. One's own experience and education
b. Experience and education available through cooperation of others (Master Mind Alliance)
c. Colleges and universities
d. Public libraries (through books and periodicals in which may be found all the knowledge organized by civilization)
e. Special training courses (through night schools and home-study schools in particular)

April 6

As knowledge is acquired it must be organized and put into use, for a definite purpose, through practical plans. Knowledge has no value except that which can be gained from its application toward some worthy end. This is one reason why college degrees are not valued more highly. They represent nothing but miscellaneous knowledge.

If you contemplate taking additional schooling, first determine the purpose for which you want the knowledge you are seeking, then learn where this particular sort of knowledge can be obtained from reliable sources.

April 7

Successful men, in all callings, never stop acquiring specialized knowledge related to their major purpose, business, or profession. Those who are not successful usually make the mistake of believing that the knowledge-acquiring period ends when one finishes school. The truth is that schooling does but little more than to put one in the way of learning how to acquire practical knowledge.

April 8

Anything acquired without effort and without cost is generally unappreciated, often discredited; perhaps this is why we get so little from our marvelous opportunity in public schools. The self-discipline one receives from a definite program of specialized study makes up, to some extent, for the wasted opportunity when knowledge was available without cost.

April 9

There is one weakness in people for which there is no remedy. It is the universal weakness of lack of ambition! Persons, especially salaried people, who schedule their spare time to provide for home study, seldom remain at the bottom very long. Their action opens the way for the upward climb, removes many obstacles from their path, and gains the friendly interest of those who have the power to put them in the way of opportunity.

The home-study method of training is especially suited to the needs of employed people who find, after leaving school, that they must acquire additional specialized knowledge but cannot spare the time to go back to school.

April 10

When a merchant finds that a certain line of merchandise is not selling, he usually supplants it with another that is in demand. The person whose business is that of marketing personal services must also be an efficient merchant. If his services do not bring adequate returns in one occupation, he must change to another, where broader opportunities are available.

April 11

The person who stops studying merely because he has finished school is forever hopelessly doomed to mediocrity, no matter what may be his calling. The way of success is the way of continuous pursuit of knowledge.

April 12

This idea of starting at the bottom and working one's way up may appear to be sound, but the major objection to it is this: Too many of those who begin at the bottom never manage to lift their heads high enough to be seen by opportunity, so they remain at the bottom. It should be remembered, also, that the outlook from the bottom is not so very bright or encouraging. It has a tendency to kill off ambition. We call it "getting into a rut," which means that we accept our fate because we form the habit of daily routine, a habit that finally becomes so strong we cease to try to throw it off. And that is another reason why it pays to start one or two steps above the bottom. By so doing one forms the habit of looking around, of observing how others get ahead, of seeing opportunity, and of embracing it without hesitation.

April 13

One of the major points I am trying to emphasize through this entire philosophy is that we rise to high positions or remain at the bottom because of conditions we can control if we desire to control them. The bottom is a monotonous, dreary, unprofitable place for any person.

I am also trying to emphasize another point, namely, that both success and failure are largely the results of habit!

April 14

There is no fixed price for sound ideas!

Back of all ideas is specialized knowledge. Unfortunately, for those who do not find riches in abundance, specialized knowledge is more abundant and more easily acquired than ideas. Because of this very truth, there is a universal demand and an ever-increasing opportunity for the person capable of helping men and women to sell their personal services advantageously. Capability means imagination, the one quality needed to combine specialized knowledge with ideas in the form of organized plans designed to yield riches.

April 15

One very common and very destructive form of lack of self-control is the habit of talking too much. People of wisdom, who know what they want and are bent on getting it, guard their conversation carefully. There can be no gain from a volume of uninvited, uncontrolled, loosely spoken words.

It is nearly always more profitable to listen than it is to speak. A good listener may, once in a great while, hear something that will add to his stock of knowledge. It requires self-control to become a good listener, but the benefits to be gained are worth the effort.

"Taking the conversation away from another person" is a common form of lack of self-control which is not only discourteous, but it deprives those who do it of many valuable opportunities to learn from others.

April 16

Life itself is a great chariot race, and the victory goes only to those who have developed the strength of character and determination and willpower to win. What matters it that we develop this strength through cruel confinement at the galley's oar, as long as we use it, so that it brings us, finally, to victory and freedom.

It is an unvarying law that strength grows out of resistance. If we pity the poor blacksmith who swings a five-pound hammer all day long, we must also admire the wonderful arm that he develops in doing it.

"Because of the dual constitution of all things, in labor as in life, there can be no cheating," says Emerson. "The thief steals from himself. The swindler swindles himself. For the real price of labor is knowledge and virtue, whereof wealth and credit are signs. The signs, like paper money, may be counterfeited or stolen, but that which they represent; namely, knowledge and virtue, cannot be counterfeited or stolen."

April 17

In searching for facts it is often necessary to gather them through the sole source of knowledge and experience of others. It then becomes necessary to examine carefully both the evidence submitted and the person from whom the evidence comes, and when the evidence is of such a nature that it affects the interest of the witness who is giving it, there will be reason to scrutinize it all the more carefully, as witnesses who have an interest in the evidence that they are submitting often yield to the temptation to color and pervert it to protect that interest.

April 18

If one man slanders another, his remarks should be accepted, if of any weight at all, with at least a grain of the proverbial salt of caution, for it is a common human tendency for men to find nothing but evil in those whom they do not like. The man who has attained to the degree of accurate thinking that enables him to speak of his enemy without exaggerating his faults and minimizing his virtues is the exception and not the rule.

Some very able men have not yet risen above this vulgar and self-destructive habit of belittling their enemies, competitors, and contemporaries. I wish to bring this common tendency to your attention with all possible emphasis, because it is a tendency that is fatal to accurate thinking.

April 19

I would direct your attention again to four major factors, with the request that you familiarize yourself with them. They are:

Auto-suggestion, the Subconscious Mind, Creative Thought, and Infinite Intelligence.

These are the four roadways over which you must travel in your upward climb in quest of knowledge. Observe that you control three of these. Observe, also—and this is especially emphasized—that upon the manner in which you traverse these three roadways will depend the time and place at which they will converge into the fourth, or Infinite Intelligence.

April 20

Let us keep in mind the fact that all success is based upon power, and power grows out of knowledge that has been organized and expressed in terms of ACTION.

The world pays for but one kind of knowledge, and that is the kind which is expressed in terms of constructive service.

April 21

As I began to reach out for knowledge in this direction and that, my mind began to unfold and broaden with such alarming rapidity that I practically found it necessary to wipe the slate of what I believed to be my previously gathered knowledge and to unlearn much that I had previously believed to be truth.

Comprehend the meaning of that which I have just stated!

April 22

TOLERANCE will teach you how to avoid the disastrous effects of racial and religious prejudices which mean defeat for millions of people who permit themselves to become entangled in foolish argument over these subjects, thereby poisoning their own minds and closing the door to reason and investigation. This lesson is the twin sister of the one on ACCURATE THOUGHT, for the reason that no one may become an Accurate Thinker without practicing tolerance. Intolerance closes the book of Knowledge and writes on the cover "Finis! I have learned it all!" Intolerance makes enemies of those who should be friends. It destroys opportunity and fills the mind with doubt, mistrust, and prejudice.

April 23

Practicing the Golden Rule will teach you how to make use of this great universal law of human conduct in such a manner that you may easily get harmonious co-operation from any individual or group of individuals. Lack of understanding of the law upon which the Golden Rule philosophy is based is one of the major causes of failure of millions of people who remain in misery, poverty, and want all their lives. This lesson has nothing whatsoever to do with religion in any form, nor with sectarianism, nor have any of the other lessons of this course on the Law of Success.

April 24

POWER is one of the three basic objects of human endeavor.

POWER is of two classes: that which is developed through coordination of natural physical laws and that which is developed by organizing and classifying KNOWLEDGE.

POWER growing out of organized knowledge is the more important, because it places in man's possession a tool with which he may transform, redirect, and to some extent harness and use the other form of power.

The object of reading this book is to mark the route by which the student may safely travel in gathering such facts as he may wish to weave into his fabric of KNOWLEDGE.

There are two major methods of gathering knowledge, namely, by studying, classifying, and assimilating facts which have been organized by other people and through one's own process of gathering, organizing, and classifying facts, generally called "personal experience."

April 25

The state of advancement known as "civilization" is but the measure of knowledge which the race has accumulated. This knowledge is of two classes: mental and physical. Among the useful knowledge organized by man, he has discovered and catalogued the eighty-odd physical elements of which all material forms in the universe consist. By study and analysis and accurate measurements man has discovered the "bigness" of the material side of the universe as represented by planets, suns, and stars, some of which are known to be over ten million times as large as the little earth on which he lives.

On the other hand, man has discovered the "littleness" of the physical forms which constitute the universe by reducing the eighty-odd physical elements to molecules, atoms, and, finally, to the smallest particle, the electron. An electron cannot be seen; it is but a center of force consisting of a positive or a negative. The electron is the beginning of everything of a physical nature.

April 26

To understand both the detail and the perspective of the process through which knowledge is gathered, organized, and classified, it seems essential to begin with the smallest and simplest particles of physical matter, because these are the ABCs with which Nature has constructed the entire framework of the physical portion of the universe.

The molecule consists of atoms, which are said to be little invisible particles of matter revolving continuously with the speed of lightning, on exactly the same principle that the earth revolves around the sun. These atoms, which revolve in one continuous circuit in the molecule, are said to be made up of electrons, the smallest particles of physical matter. The electron is uniform, thus in a grain of sand or a drop of water the entire principle upon which the whole universe operates is duplicated.

How marvelous! How stupendous! You may gather some slight idea of the magnitude of it all the next time you eat a meal, by remembering that every article of food you eat, the plate on which you eat it, the tableware, and the table itself are, in final analysis, but a collection of ELECTRONS.

April 27

In speaking of the source of his great storehouse of knowledge, Thomas Paine thus described it:

"Any person, who has made observations on the state of progress of the human mind, by observing his own, cannot but have observed that there are two distinct classes of what are called Thoughts: those that we produce in ourselves by reflection and the act of thinking, and those that bolt into the mind of their own accord. I have always made it a rule to treat these voluntary visitors with civility, taking care to examine, as well as I was able, if they were worth entertaining; and it is from them I have acquired almost all the knowledge that I have. As to the learning that any person gains from school education, it serves only like a small capital, to put him in the way of beginning learning for himself afterwards. Every person of learning is finally his own teacher, the reason for which is, that principles cannot be impressed upon the memory; their place of mental residence is the understanding, and they are never so lasting as when they begin by conception."

April 28

Most of the useful knowledge to which the human race has become heir has been preserved and accurately recorded in Nature's Bible. By turning back the pages of this unalterable Bible, man has read the story of the terrific struggle through and out of which the present civilization has grown. The pages of this Bible are made up of the physical elements of which this earth and the other planets consist, and of the ether which fills all space.

By turning back the pages written on stone and covered near the surface of this earth, man has uncovered the bones, skeletons, footprints, and other unmistakable evidence of the history of animal life, planted there for his enlightenment and guidance by the hand of Mother Nature throughout time. The evidence is plain and unmistakable. The great stone pages of Nature's Bible found on this earth and the endless pages of that Bible wherein all past human thought has been recorded constitute an authentic source of communication between the Creator and man. This Bible was begun before man had reached the thinking stage; indeed, before man had reached the amœba (one-cell animal) stage of development.

April 29

Every mind, or brain, is directly connected with every other brain by means of the ether. Every thought released by any brain may be instantly picked up and interpreted by all other brains that are "en rapport" with the sending brain. This author is as sure of this fact as he is that the chemical formula H_2O will produce water. Imagine, if you can, what a part this principle plays in every walk of life.

April 30

Remember, the IDEA is the main thing. Specialized knowledge may be found just around the corner—any corner!

MAY

The Fifth Step Toward Riches

IMAGINATION

May 1

The imagination is literally the workshop wherein are fashioned all plans created by man. The impulse, the desire, is given shape, form, and action through the aid of the imaginative faculty of the mind.

It has been said that man can create anything which he can imagine.

May 2

Through the aid of his imaginative faculty, man has discovered, and harnessed, more of Nature's forces during the past fifty years than during the entire history of the human race previous to that time.

Man's only limitation, within reason, lies in his development and use of his imagination. He has not yet reached the apex of development in the use of his imaginative faculty. He has merely discovered that he has an imagination and has commenced to use it in a very elementary way.

May 3

The imaginative faculty functions in two forms: One is known as "synthetic imagination" and the other as "creative imagination."

Synthetic Imagination: Through this faculty, one may arrange old concepts, ideas, or plans into new combinations. This faculty *creates* nothing. It merely works with the material of experience, education, and observation with which it is fed. It is the faculty used most by the inventor, with the exception of the "genius" who draws upon the creative imagination when he cannot solve his problem through synthetic imagination.

May 4

reative Imagination: Through the faculty of creative imagination, the finite mind of man has direct communication with Infinite Intelligence. It is the faculty through which "hunches" and "inspirations" are received. It is by this faculty that all basic or new ideas are handed over to man. It is through this faculty that thought vibrations from the minds of others are received. It is through this faculty that one individual may "tune in," or communicate with, the subconscious minds of other men.

May 5

The creative imagination works automatically. This faculty functions only when the conscious mind is vibrating at an exceedingly rapid rate, as for example, when the conscious mind is stimulated through the emotion of a *strong desire*.

The creative faculty becomes more alert, more receptive to vibrations from the sources mentioned in proportion to its development through use. This statement is significant! Ponder over it before passing on.

May 6

The great leaders of business, industry, and finance, and the great artists, musicians, poets, and writers became great because they developed the faculty of creative imagination.

Both the synthetic and creative faculties of imagination become more alert with use, just as any muscle or organ of the body develops through use.

May 7

Desire is only a thought, an impulse. It is nebulous and ephemeral. It is abstract and of no value until it has been transformed into its physical counterpart. While the synthetic imagination is the one which will be used most frequently in the process of transforming the impulse of desire into money, you must keep in mind the fact that you may face circumstances and situations which demand use of the creative imagination as well.

Your imaginative faculty may have become weak through inaction. It can be revived and made alert through use. This faculty does not die, though it may become quiescent through lack of use.

May 8

Center your attention, for the time being, on the development of the synthetic imagination, because this is the faculty which you will use more often in the process of converting desire into money. Transformation of the intangible impulse, of desire, into the tangible reality of money calls for the use of a plan or plans. These plans must be formed with the aid of the imagination and mainly with the synthetic faculty.

Begin at once to put your imagination to work on the building of a plan or plans for the transformation of your desire into money. Reduce your plan to writing, if you have not already done so. The moment you complete this, you will have definitely given concrete form to the intangible desire. Read the preceding sentence once more. Read it aloud very slowly, and, as you do so, remember that the moment you reduce the statement of your desire, and a plan for its realization, to writing, you have actually taken the first of a series of steps which will enable you to convert the thought into its physical counterpart.

May 9

The earth on which you live, you, yourself, and every other material thing are the result of evolutionary change, through which microscopic bits of matter have been organized and arranged in an orderly fashion.

Moreover—and this statement is of stupendous importance—this earth, every one of the billions of individual cells of your body, and every atom of matter *began as an intangible form of energy.*

May 10

Desire is thought impulse! Thought impulses are forms of energy. When you begin with the thought impulse, or desire, to accumulate money, you are drafting into your service the same "stuff" that Nature used in creating this earth and every material form in the universe, including the body and brain in which the thought impulses function.

May 11

As far as science has been able to determine, the entire universe consists of but two elements—matter and energy. Through the combination of energy and matter has been created everything perceptible to man, from the largest star which floats in the heavens down to, and including, man himself.

You are now engaged in the task of trying to profit by Nature's method. You are (sincerely and earnestly, we hope) trying to adapt yourself to Nature's laws, by endeavoring to convert desire into its physical or monetary equivalent. You can do it! It has been done before!

May 12

You can build a fortune through the aid of laws which are immutable. But, first, you must become familiar with these laws and learn to use them. Through repetition, and by approaching the description of these principles from every conceivable angle, the author hopes to reveal to you the secret through which every great fortune has been accumulated.

May 13

God seems to throw Himself on the side of the man who knows *exactly* what he wants, *if he is determined* to get just that!

If you are one of those who believe that hard work and honesty, alone, will bring riches, perish the thought! It is not true! Riches, when they come in huge quantities, are never the result of hard work! Riches come, if they come at all, in response to definite demands based upon the application of definite principles and not by chance or luck.

May 14

Generally speaking, an idea is an impulse of thought that impels action by an appeal to the imagination. All master salesmen know that ideas can be sold where merchandise cannot. Ordinary salesmen do not know this—that is why they are "ordinary."

May 15

Millions of people go through life hoping for favorable "breaks." Perhaps a favorable break can get one an opportunity, but the safest plan is not to depend upon luck. It was a favorable "break" that gave me the biggest opportunity of my life—*but*—twenty-five years of *determined effort* had to be devoted to that opportunity before it became an asset.

The "break" consisted of my good fortune in meeting and gaining the cooperation of Andrew Carnegie. On that occasion Carnegie planted in my mind the *idea* of organizing the principles of achievement into a philosophy of success. Thousands of people have profited by the discoveries made in the twenty-five years of research, and several fortunes have been accumulated through the application of the philosophy. The beginning was simple. It was an idea which anyone might have developed.

The favorable break came through Carnegie, but what about the determination, definiteness of purpose, and the desire to attain the goal, and the persistent effort of twenty-five years? It was no ordinary desire that survived disappointment, discouragement, temporary defeat, criticism, and the constant reminding of "waste of time." It was a burning desire! An obsession!

May 16

When the idea was first planted in my mind by Mr. Carnegie, it was coaxed, nursed, and enticed to *remain alive*. Gradually, the idea became a giant under its own power, and it coaxed, nursed, and drove me. Ideas are like that. First you give life and action and guidance to ideas, and then they take on power of their own and sweep aside all opposition.

May 17

Ideas are intangible forces, but they have more power than the physical brains that give birth to them. They have the power to live on after the brain that creates them has returned to dust. For example, take the power of Christianity. That began with a simple idea born in the brain of Christ. Its chief tenet was "Do unto others as you would have others do unto you." Christ has gone back to the source from whence He came, but His idea goes marching on. Some day it may grow up and come into its own; then it will have fulfilled Christ's deepest desire. The idea has been developing for only two thousand years. Give it time!

May 18

IMAGINATION will stimulate your mind so that you will conceive new ideas and develop new plans which will help you in attaining the object of your Definite Chief Aim. It will teach you how to "build new houses out of old stones," so to speak. It will show you how to create new ideas out of old, well-known concepts and how to put old ideas to new uses. This one lesson, alone, is the equivalent of a very practical course in salesmanship, and it is sure to prove a veritable gold mine of knowledge to the person who is in earnest.

May 19

Formation of the Habit of Saving does not mean that you shall limit your earning capacity; it means just the opposite—that you shall apply this law so that it not only conserves that which you earn, in a systematic manner, but it also places you in the way of greater opportunity and gives you the vision, the self-confidence, the imagination, the enthusiasm, the initiative, and leadership actually to increase your earning capacity.

Stating this great law in another way, when you thoroughly understand the Law of Habit you may ensure yourself success in the great game of moneymaking by "playing both ends of that game against the middle."

May 20

Every Leader makes use of the Law of a Definite Purpose, the Law of Self-confidence, and the Law of Initiative and Leadership. And if he is an outstanding, successful Leader he makes use, also, of the laws of Imagination, Enthusiasm, Self-Control, Pleasing Personality, Accurate Thinking, Concentration, and Tolerance. Without the combined use of all these laws no one may become a really great Leader. Omission of a single one of these laws lessens the power of the Leader proportionately.

May 21

S*uccess*, no matter what may be one's conception of that term, is nearly always a question of one's ability to get others to subordinate their own individualities and follow a Leader. The Leader who has the Personality and the Imagination to induce his followers to accept his plans and carry them out faithfully is always an able Leader.

Leadership and Imagination are so closely allied and so essential for success that one cannot be successfully applied without the other. Initiative is the moving force that pushes the Leader ahead, but Imagination is the guiding spirit that tells him which way to go.

May 22

Perhaps one of the most important advantages of Imagination is that it enables one to separate all problems into their component parts and to reassemble them in more favorable combinations.

It has been said that all battles in warfare are won or lost not on the firing line after the battle begins but back of the lines, through the sound strategy, or the lack of it, used by the generals who plan the battles.

What is true of warfare is equally true in business, and in most other problems which confront us throughout life. We win or lose according to the nature of the plans we build and carry out, a fact which serves to emphasize the value of the laws of Initiative and Leadership, Imagination, Self-confidence, and a Definite Chief Aim. With the intelligent use of these four laws, one may build plans for any purpose whatsoever which cannot be defeated by any person or group of persons who do not employ or understand these laws.

There is no escape from the truth here stated!

May 23

ORGANIZED EFFORT is effort which is directed according to a plan that was conceived with the aid of Imagination, guided by a Definite Chief Aim, and given momentum with Initiative and Self-confidence. These laws blend into one and become a power in the hands of a Leader. Without their aid, effective leadership is impossible.

May 24

Imagination is the workshop of the human mind wherein old ideas and established facts may be re-assembled into new combinations and put to new uses. The dictionary defines *imagination* as follows:

> The act of constructive intellect in grouping the materials of knowledge or thought into new, original and rational systems; the constructive or creative faculty; embracing poetic, artistic, philosophic, scientific and ethical imagination.
>
> The picturing power of the mind; the formation of mental images, pictures, or mental representation of objects or ideas, particularly of objects of sense perception and of mathematical reasoning! also the reproduction and combination, usually with more or less irrational or abnormal modification, of the images or ideas of memory or recalled facts of experience.

May 25

Imagination has been called the creative power of the soul, but this is somewhat abstract and goes more deeply into the meaning than is necessary from the viewpoint of a student of this course who wishes to use the course only as a means of attaining material or monetary advantages in life.

If you have mastered and thoroughly understood the preceding lessons of this book, you know that the materials out of which you built your definite chief aim were assembled and combined in your imagination. You also know that self-confidence and initiative and leadership must be created in your imagination before they can become a reality, for it is in the workshop of your imagination that you will put the principle of auto-suggestion into operation in creating these necessary qualities.

May 26

You will never have a definite purpose in life, you will never have self-confidence, you will never have initiative and leadership unless you first create these qualities in your imagination and see yourself in possession of them.

Just as the oak tree develops from the germ that lies in the acorn, and the bird develops from the germ that lies asleep in the egg, so will your material achievements grow out of the organized plans that you create in your imagination. First comes the thought, then organization of that thought into ideas and plans, then transformation of those plans into reality. The beginning, as you will observe, is in your imagination.

May 27

The imagination is both interpretative and creative in nature. It can examine facts, concepts, and ideas, and it can create new combinations and plans out of these.

Through its interpretative capacity the imagination has one power not generally attributed to it, namely, the power to register vibrations and thought waves that are put into motion from outside sources, just as the radio-receiving apparatus picks up the vibrations of sound. The principle through which this interpretative capacity of the imagination functions is called telepathy, the communication of thought from one mind to another, at long or short distances, without the aid of physical or mechanical appliances.

May 28

The imagination is too often regarded merely as an indefinite, untraceable, indescribable something that does nothing but create fiction. It is this popular disregard of the powers of the imagination that has made necessary these more or less abstract references to one of the most important subjects of this course. Not only is the subject of imagination an important factor, but it is one of the most interesting subjects, as you will observe when you begin to see how it affects all that you do toward the achievement of your Definite Chief Aim.

May 29

You will see how important is the subject of imagination when you stop to realize that it is the only thing in the world over which you have absolute control. Others may deprive you of your material wealth and cheat you in a thousand ways, but no man can deprive you of the control and use of your imagination. Men may deal with you unfairly, as men often do; they may deprive you of your liberty, but they cannot take from you the privilege of using your imagination as you wish.

May 30

The major trouble with this world today lies in our lack of understanding of the power of imagination, for if we understood this great power we could use it as a weapon with which to wipe out poverty and misery and injustice and persecution, and this could be done in a single generation.

May 31

Success requires no explanations; failure permits no alibis.

JUNE

The Sixth Step Toward Riches

ORGANIZED PLANNING

June 1

How to build plans which will be practical:

a. Ally yourself with a group of as many people as you may need for the creation and carrying out of your plan or plans for the accumulation of money—making use of the Master Mind principle. (Compliance with this instruction is *absolutely essential*. Do not neglect it.)

b. Before forming your Master Mind alliance, decide what advantages and benefits *you* may offer the individual members of your group in return for their cooperation. No one will work indefinitely without some form of compensation. No intelligent person will either request or expect another to work without adequate compensation, although this may not always be in the form of money.

c. Arrange to meet with the members of your Master Mind group at least twice a week, and more often if possible, until you have jointly perfected the necessary plan or plans for the accumulation of money.

d. Maintain perfect harmony between yourself and every member of your Master Mind group. If you fail to carry out this instruction to the letter, you may expect to meet with failure. The Master Mind principle *cannot* obtain where perfect harmony does not prevail.

June 2

Keep in mind these facts:

First, you are engaged in an undertaking of major importance to you. To be sure of success, you must have plans which are faultless.

Second, you must have the advantage of the experience, education, native ability, and imagination of other minds. This is in harmony with the methods followed by every person who has accumulated a great fortune.

June 3

When you begin to select members for your Master Mind group, endeavor to select those who do not take defeat seriously.

No individual has sufficient experience, education, native ability, and knowledge to ensure the accumulation of a great fortune without the cooperation of other people. Every plan you adopt in your endeavor to accumulate wealth should be the joint creation of yourself and every other member of your Master Mind group. You may originate your own plans, either in whole or in part, but see that those plans are checked and approved by the members of your Master Mind alliance.

June 4

If the first plan which you adopt does not work success-fully, replace it with a new plan; if this new plan fails to work, replace it in turn with still another, and so on, until you find a plan which does work. Right here is the point at which the majority of men meet with failure, because of their lack of persistence in creating new plans to take the place of those which fail.

The most intelligent man living cannot succeed in accumulating money—nor in any other undertaking—without plans which are practical and workable. Just keep this fact in mind, and remember when your plans fail that temporary defeat is not permanent failure. It may only mean that your plans have not been sound. Build other plans. Start all over again.

June 5

Thomas A. Edison "failed" ten thousand times before he perfected the incandescent electric light bulb. That is, he met with *temporary defeat* ten thousand times before his efforts were crowned with success.

Temporary defeat should mean only one thing: the certain knowledge that there is something wrong with your plan. Millions of men go through life in misery and poverty, because they lack a sound plan through which to accumulate a fortune.

Henry Ford accumulated a fortune, not because of his superior mind but because he adopted and followed a plan which proved to be sound. A thousand men could be pointed out, each with a better education than Ford's, yet each of whom lives in poverty because he does not possess the right plan for the accumulation of money.

June 6

Your achievement can be no greater than your plans are sound. That may seem to be an axiomatic statement, but it is true.

No man is ever whipped until he quits—*in his own mind.*

This fact will be repeated many times, because it is so easy to "take the count" at the first sign of defeat.

James J. Hill met with temporary defeat when he first endeavored to raise the necessary capital to build a railroad from the East to the West, but he, too, turned defeat into victory *through new plans.*

Henry Ford met with temporary defeat not only at the beginning of his automobile career but after he had gone far toward the top. He created new plans and went marching on to financial victory.

We see men who have accumulated great fortunes, but we often recognize only their triumph, overlooking the temporary defeats which they had to surmount before "arriving."

June 7

No follower of this philosophy can reasonably expect to accumulate a fortune without experiencing "temporary defeat." When defeat comes, accept it as a signal that your plans are not sound, rebuild those plans, and set sail once more toward your coveted goal. If you give up before your goal has been reached, you are a "quitter."

**A quitter never wins—and—a
winner never quits.**

Lift this sentence out, write it on a piece of paper in letters an inch high, and place it where you will see it every night before you go to sleep and every morning before you go to work.

June 8

Some people foolishly believe that only money can make money. This is not true! Desire, transmuted into its monetary equivalent through the principles laid down here, is the agency through which money is "made." Money, of itself, is nothing but inert matter. It cannot move, think, or talk, but it can "hear" when a man who desires it calls it to come!

Intelligent planning is essential for success in any undertaking designed to accumulate riches. It should be encouraging to know that practically all the great fortunes began in the form of compensation for personal services or from the sale of ideas. What else, except ideas and personal services, would one not possessed of property have to give in return for riches?

June 9

Broadly speaking, there are two types of people in the world: One type is known as leaders, and the other as followers. Decide at the outset whether you intend to become a leader in your chosen calling or remain a follower. The difference in compensation is vast. The follower cannot reasonably expect the compensation to which a leader is entitled, although many followers make the mistake of expecting such pay.

It is no disgrace to be a follower. On the other hand, it is no credit to remain a follower. Most great leaders began in the capacity of followers. They became great leaders because they were intelligent followers. With few exceptions, the man who cannot follow a leader intelligently cannot become an efficient leader. The man who can follow a leader most efficiently is usually the man who develops into leadership most rapidly. An intelligent follower has many advantages, among them the opportunity to acquire knowledge from his leader.

June 10

The following are important factors of leadership:

1. Unwavering courage based upon knowledge of self and of one's occupation.
2. Self-control.
3. A keen sense of justice.
4. Definiteness of decision.
5. Definiteness of plans.
6. The habit of doing more than paid for.
7. A pleasing personality.
8. Sympathy and understanding.
9. Mastery of detail.
10. Willingness to assume full responsibility.
11. Cooperation.

June 11

There are two forms of Leadership. The first, and by far the most effective, is leadership of consent of, and with the sympathy of, the followers. The second is leadership by force, without the consent and sympathy of the followers. History is filled with evidences that Leadership by Force cannot endure. The downfall and disappearance of dictators and kings is significant. It means that people will not follow forced leadership indefinitely.

Those who belong to the old school of Leadership by Force must acquire an understanding of the new brand of leadership (cooperation) or be relegated to the rank and file of the followers. There is no other way out for them.

Leadership by Consent of the followers is the only brand which can endure!

June 12

THE TEN MAJOR CAUSES OF FAILURE
IN LEADERSHIP

We come now to the major faults of leaders who fail, because it is just as essential to know what not to do as it is to know what to do.

1. *Inability to organize details.* Efficient leadership calls for ability to organize and to master details. No genuine leader is ever "too busy" to do anything which may be required of him in his capacity as leader. When a man, whether he is a leader or follower, admits that he is "too busy" to change his plans, or to give attention to any emergency, he admits his inefficiency. The successful leader must be the master of all details connected with his position. That means, of course, that he must acquire the habit of relegating details to capable lieutenants.

June 13

THE TEN MAJOR CAUSES OF FAILURE
IN LEADERSHIP
(continued)

2. *Unwillingness to render humble service.* Truly great leaders are willing, when occasion demands, to perform any sort of labor which they would ask another to perform. "The greatest among ye shall be the servant of all" is a truth which all able leaders observe and respect.

June 14

THE 10 MAJOR CAUSES OF FAILURE IN LEADERSHIP
(continued)

3. *Expectation of pay for what they "know" instead of what they do with that which they know.* The world does not pay men for that which they "know." It pays them for what they DO or induce others to do.

June 15

THE TEN MAJOR CAUSES OF FAILURE
IN LEADERSHIP
(continued)

4. *Fear of competition from followers.* The leader who fears that one of his followers may take his position is practically sure to realize that fear sooner or later. The able leader trains understudies to whom he may delegate, at will, any of the details of his position. Only in this way may a leader multiply himself and prepare himself to be at many places and give attention to many things at one time. It is an eternal truth that men receive more pay for their ability to get others to perform than they could possibly earn by their own efforts. An efficient leader may, through his knowledge of his job and the magnetism of his personality, greatly increase the efficiency of others and induce them to render more service and better service than they could render without his aid.

June 16

THE TEN MAJOR CAUSES OF FAILURE
IN LEADERSHIP
(continued)

5. *Lack of imagination.* Without imagination, the leader is incapable of meeting emergencies and of creating plans by which to guide his followers efficiently.

June 17

THE TEN MAJOR CAUSES OF FAILURE
IN LEADERSHIP
(continued)

6. *Selfishness.* The leader who claims all the
   honor for the work of his followers is sure
   to be met by resentment. The really great
   leader claims none of the honors. He is con-
   tented to see the honors, when there are
   any, go to his followers, because he knows
   that most men will work harder for com-
   mendation and recognition than they will
   for money alone.

June 18

THE TEN MAJOR CAUSES OF FAILURE IN LEADERSHIP
(continued)

7. *Intemperance.* Followers do not respect an intemperate leader. Moreover, intemperance in any of its various forms destroys the endurance and the vitality of all who indulge in it.

June 19

THE TEN MAJOR CAUSES OF FAILURE
IN LEADERSHIP
(continued)

8. *Disloyalty.* Perhaps this should have come at the head of the list. The leader who is not loyal to his trust, and to his associates, those above him, and those below him, cannot long maintain his leadership. Disloyalty marks one as being less than the dust of the earth and brings down on one's head the contempt he deserves. Lack of loyalty is one of the major causes of failure in every walk of life.

June 20

THE TEN MAJOR CAUSES OF FAILURE IN LEADERSHIP
(continued)

9. *Emphasis of the "authority" of leadership.* The efficient leader leads by encouraging and not by trying to instill fear in the hearts of his followers. The leader who tries to impress his followers with his "authority" comes within the category of leadership through force. If a leader is a real leader, he will have no need to advertise that fact except by his conduct—his sympathy, understanding, fairness, and a demonstration that he knows his job.

June 21

THE TEN MAJOR CAUSES OF FAILURE
IN LEADERSHIP
(continued)

10. *Emphasis of title.* The competent leader requires no "title" to give him the respect of his followers. The man who makes too much over his title generally has little else to emphasize. The doors to the office of the real leader are open to all who wish to enter, and his working quarters are free from formality or ostentation.

These are among the more common of the causes of failure in leadership. Any one of these faults is sufficient to induce failure. Study the list carefully if you aspire to leadership, and make sure that you are free of these faults.

June 22

Everyone enjoys doing the kind of work for which he is best suited. An artist loves to work with paints, a craftsman with his hands, a writer loves to write. Those with less definite talents have their preferences for certain fields of business and industry. If America does anything well, it offers a full range of occupations. Decide exactly what kind of a job you want. If the job doesn't already exist, perhaps you can create it.

Every person who starts or "gets in" halfway up the ladder does so by deliberate and careful planning.

June 23

Men and women who market their services to best advantage in the future must recognize the stupendous change which has taken place in connection with the relationship between employer and employee.

In the future, the Golden Rule, and not the "Rule of Gold," will be the dominating factor in the marketing of merchandise as well as personal services. The future relationship between employers and their employees will be more in the nature of a partnership consisting of:

a. The employer
b. The employee
c. The public they serve

The real employer of the future will be the public. This should be kept uppermost in mind by every person seeking to market personal services effectively. The "public-be-damned" policy is now passé. It has been supplanted by the "we-are-obligingly-at-your-service, sir" policy.

June 24

Courtesy and *Service* are the watchwords of merchandising today and apply to the person who is marketing personal services even more directly than to the employer whom he serves, because, in the final analysis, both the employer and his employee are employed by the public they serve. If they fail to serve well, they pay by the loss of their privilege of serving.

June 25

The wages of sin is death!" Many have read this in the Bible, but few have discovered its meaning. Now, and for several years, the entire world has been listening by force to a sermon which might well be called "Whatsoever a man soweth, that shall he also reap."

Nothing as widespread and effective as the depression could possibly be "just a coincidence." Behind the depression was a cause. Nothing ever happens without a cause. In the main, the cause of the depression is traceable directly to the worldwide habit of trying to reap without sowing.

If there is a principle of cause and effect, which controls business, finance, and transportation, this same principle controls individuals and determines their economic status.

June 26

The causes of success in marketing services effectively and permanently have been clearly described. Unless those causes are studied, analyzed, understood, and applied, no man can market his services effectively and permanently. Every person must be his own salesman of personal services. The quality and the quantity of service rendered, and the spirit in which it is rendered, determine to a large extent the price and the duration of employment. To market personal services effectively (which means a permanent market, at a satisfactory price, under pleasant conditions), one must adopt and follow the "QQS" formula, which means that Quality plus Quantity plus the proper Spirit of cooperation equal perfect salesmanship of service. Remember the QQS formula, but do more—apply it as a habit!

June 27

Let us analyze the QQS formula to make sure we understand exactly what it means.

1. *Quality* of service shall be construed to mean the performance of every detail, in connection with your position, in the most efficient manner possible, with the object of greater efficiency always in mind.

2. *Quantity* of service shall be understood to mean the habit of rendering all the service of which you are capable, at all times, with the purpose of increasing the amount of service rendered as greater skill is developed through practice and experience. Emphasis is again placed on the word *habit*.

3. *Spirit* of service shall be construed to mean the habit of agreeable, harmonious conduct which will induce cooperation from associates and fellow employees.

Adequacy of quality and quantity of service is not sufficient to maintain a permanent market for your services. The conduct, or the spirit in which you deliver service, is a strong determining factor in connection with both the price you receive and the duration of employment.

June 28

The importance of a pleasing personality has been stressed because it is a factor which enables one to render service in the proper spirit. If one has a personality which pleases, and renders service in a spirit of harmony, these assets often make up for deficiencies in both the quality and the quantity of service one renders. Nothing, however, can be successfully substituted for pleasing conduct.

June 29

The person whose income is derived entirely from the sale of personal services is no less a merchant than the man who sells commodities, and it might well be added, such a person is subject to exactly the same rules of conduct as the merchant who sells merchandise.

This has been emphasized because the majority of people who live by the sale of personal services make the mistake of considering themselves free from the rules of conduct and the responsibilities attached to those who are engaged in marketing commodities.

The new way of marketing services has practically forced both employer and employee into partnership alliances through which both take into consideration the rights of the third party, the public they serve.

June 30

The day of the "go-getter" has passed. He has been supplanted by the "go-giver." High-pressure methods in business finally blew the lid off. There will never be the need to put the lid back on, because, in the future, business will be conducted by methods that will require no pressure.

The actual capital value of your brains may be determined by the amount of income you can produce (by marketing your services). Money is worth no more than brains. It is often worth much less. Competent "brains," if effectively marketed, represent a much more desirable form of capital than that which is required to conduct a business dealing in commodities, because "brains" are a form of capital which cannot be permanently depreciated through depressions, nor can this form of capital be stolen or spent. Moreover, the money which is essential for the conduct of business is as worthless as a sand dune until it has been mixed with efficient "brains."

JULY

The Seventh Step Toward Riches

DECISION

July 1

Accurate analysis of over 25,000 men and women who had experienced failure disclosed the fact that lack of decision was near the head of the list of the thirty major causes of failure. This is no mere statement of a theory; *it is a fact*.

Procrastination, the opposite of decision, is a common enemy which practically every man must conquer.

You will have an opportunity to test your capacity to reach *quick* and *definite* decisions when you finish reading this book and are ready to begin putting into action the principles which it describes.

July 2

Analysis of several hundred people who had accumulated fortunes well beyond the million-dollar mark disclosed the fact that *every one of them* had the habit of reaching decisions promptly and of changing these decisions slowly if and when they were changed. People who fail to accumulate money, *without exception,* have the habit of reaching decisions, if at all, very *slowly* and of *changing these decisions quickly and often.*

July 3

The majority of people who fail to accumulate money sufficient for their needs are, generally, easily influenced by the "opinions" of others. They permit the newspapers and the "gossiping" neighbors to do their "thinking" for them. "Opinions" are the cheapest commodities on earth. Everyone has a flock of opinions ready to be wished upon anyone who will accept them. If you are influenced by "opinions" when you reach decisions, you will not succeed in any undertaking, much less in that of transmuting your own desire into money.

July 4

If you are influenced by the opinions of others, you will have no desire of your own.

Keep your own counsel when you begin to put into practice the principles described here by *reaching your own decisions* and following them. Take no one into your confidence, except the members of your Master Mind group, and be very sure in your selection of this group, that you choose only those who will be in complete sympathy and harmony with your purpose.

July 5

Close friends and relatives, while not meaning to do so, often handicap one through "opinions" and sometimes through ridicule, which is meant to be humorous. Thousands of men and women carry inferiority complexes with them all through life, because some well-meaning but ignorant person destroyed their confidence through "opinions" or ridicule.

July 6

You have a brain and mind of your own. Use it, and reach your own decisions. If you need facts or information from other people to enable you to reach decisions, as you probably will in many instances, acquire these facts or secure the information you need quietly, without disclosing your purpose.

July 7

It is characteristic of people who have but a smattering or a veneer of knowledge to try to give the impression that they have much knowledge. Such people generally do too much talking and too little listening. Keep your eyes and ears wide open—and your mouth closed—if you wish to acquire the habit of prompt decision. Those who talk too much do little else. If you talk more than you listen, you not only deprive yourself of many opportunities to accumulate useful knowledge, but you also disclose your plans and purposes to people who will take great delight in defeating you, because they envy you.

Remember, also, that every time you open your mouth in the presence of a person who has an abundance of knowledge, you display to that person your exact stock of knowledge—or your lack of it! Genuine wisdom is usually conspicuous through *modesty and silence.*

July 8

Keep in mind the fact that every person with whom you associate is, like yourself, seeking the opportunity to accumulate money. If you talk about your plans too freely, you may be surprised when you learn that some other person has beaten you to your goal by putting into action ahead of you the plans of which you talked unwisely.

Let one of your first decisions be to keep a closed mouth and open ears and eyes.

As a reminder to yourself to follow this advice, it will be helpful if you copy the following epigram in large letters and place it where you will see it daily: "Tell the world what you intend to do, but first show it." This is the equivalent of saying that "deeds, and not words, are what count most."

July 9

The value of decisions depends upon the courage required to render them. The great decisions which served as the foundation of civilization were reached by assuming great risks, which often meant the possibility of death.

The greatest decision of all time, as far as any American citizen is concerned, was reached in Philadelphia, July 4, 1776, when fifty-six men signed their names to a document, which they well knew would bring freedom to all Americans or *leave every one of the fifty-six hanging from a gallows!*

July 10

Analyze the events which led to the Declaration of Independence, and be convinced that this nation, which now holds a position of commanding respect and power among all nations of the world, was born of a decision created by a Master Mind consisting of fifty-six men. Note well the fact that it was their decision which ensured the success of Washington's armies, because the *spirit* of that decision was in the heart of every soldier who fought with him and served as a spiritual power which recognizes no such thing as failure.

Note, also (with great personal benefit) that the power which gave this nation its freedom, is the self-same power that must be used by every individual who becomes self-determining. This power is made up of the principles described in this book. It will not be difficult to detect in the story of the Declaration of Independence at least six of these principles: desire, decision, faith, persistence, the Master Mind, and organized planning.

July 11

Throughout this philosophy will be found the suggestion that thought, backed by strong desire, has a tendency to transmute itself into its physical equivalent.

In your search for the secret of the method, do not look for a miracle, because you will not find it. You will find only the eternal laws of Nature. These laws are available to every person who has the faith and the courage to use them. They may be used to bring freedom to a nation or to accumulate riches. There is no charge save the time necessary to understand and appropriate them.

July 12

Those who reach decisions promptly and definitely know what they want, and generally get it. The leaders in every walk of life decide quickly and firmly. That is the major reason why they are leaders. The world has the habit of making room for the man whose words and actions show that he knows where he is going.

July 13

Indecision is a habit which usually begins in youth. The habit takes on permanency as the youth goes through grade school, high school, and even through college without definiteness of purpose. The major weakness of all educational systems is that they neither teach nor encourage the habit of definite decision.

The habit of indecision acquired because of the deficiencies of our school systems goes with the student into the occupation he chooses . . . if . . . in fact, he chooses his occupation. Generally, the youth just out of school seeks any job that can be found. He takes the first place he finds, because he has fallen into the habit of indecision. Ninety-eight out of every hundred people working for wages today are in the positions they hold, because they lacked the definiteness of decision to plan a definite position and the knowledge of how to choose an employer.

July 14

Definiteness of decision always requires courage, sometimes very great courage. The fifty-six men who signed the Declaration of Independence staked their lives on the decision to affix their signatures to that document. The person who reaches a definite decision to procure the particular job and make life pay the price he asks does not stake his life on that decision; he stakes his economic freedom. Financial independence, riches, desirable business and professional positions are not within reach of the person who neglects or refuses to expect, plan, and demand these things. The person who desires riches in the same spirit that Samuel Adams desired freedom for the Colonies, is sure to accumulate wealth.

July 15

If success depends upon power, and if power is organized effort, and if the first step in the direction of organization is a definite purpose, then one may easily see why such a purpose is essential.

Until a man selects a definite purpose in life he dissipates his energies and spreads his thoughts over so many subjects and in so many different directions that they lead not to power but to indecision and weakness.

July 16

Careful observation of the business philosophy of more than one hundred men and women who have attained outstanding success in their respective callings disclosed the fact that each was a person of prompt and definite decision.

The habit of working with a Definite Chief Aim will breed in you the habit of prompt decision, and this habit will come to your aid in all that you do.

July 17

The habit of working with a Definite Chief Aim will help you to concentrate all your attention on any given task until you have mastered it. Concentration of effort and the habit of working with a Definite Chief Aim are two of the essential factors in success which are always found together. One leads to the other.

July 18

I t requires force of character, determination, and power of firm DECISION to open a savings account and then add to it a regular, if small, portion of all subsequent income.

There is one rule by which any man may determine, well in advance, whether or not he will ever enjoy the financial freedom and independence which is so universally desired by all men, and this rule has absolutely nothing to do with the amount of one's income. The rule is that if a man follows the systematic habit of saving a definite proportion of all money he earns or receives in other ways, he is practically sure to place himself in a position of financial independence. If he saves nothing, he IS ABSOLUTELY SURE NEVER TO BE FINANCIALLY INDEPENDENT, no matter how much his income may be.

July 19

Y ou are not making the most of this book if you do not take some step each day that brings you nearer realization of your Definite Chief Aim. Do not fool yourself or permit yourself to be misled to believe that the object of your Definite Chief Aim will materialize if you only wait. The materialization will come through your own determination, backed by your own carefully laid plans and your own initiative in putting those plans into action, or it will not come at all.

One of the major requisites for Leadership is the power of quick and firm DECISION!

Analysis of more than 16,000 people disclosed the fact that Leaders are always men of ready decision, even in matters of small importance, while the follower is NEVER a person of quick decision. This is worth remembering!

July 20

The follower, in whatever walk of life you find him, is a man who seldom knows what he wants. He vacillates, procrastinates, and actually refuses to reach a decision, even in matters of the smallest importance, unless a Leader induces him to do so.

To know that the majority of people cannot and will not reach decisions quickly, if at all, is of great help to the Leader who knows what he wants and has a plan for getting it.

July 21

The Leader not only works with A DEFINITE CHIEF AIM, but he has a very definite plan for attaining the object of that aim. It will be seen, also, that the Law of Self-confidence becomes an important part of the working equipment of the Leader.

The chief reason why the follower does not reach decisions is that he lacks the Self-confidence to do so.

July 22

The selection of a Definite Chief Aim calls for the use of both imagination and decision! The power of decision grows with use. Prompt decision in forcing the imagination to create a Definite Chief Aim renders more powerful the capacity to reach decisions in other matters.

Adversities and temporary defeat are generally blessings in disguise, for the reason that they force one to use both imagination and decision. This is why a man usually makes a better fight when his back is to the wall and he knows there is no retreat. He then reaches the decision to fight instead of running.

July 23

The imagination is never quite so active as it is when one faces some emergency calling for quick and definite decision and action. In these moments of emergency men have reached decisions, built plans, used their imagination in such a manner that they became known as genii. Many a genius has been born out of the necessity for unusual stimulation of the imagination, as the result of some trying experience which forced quick thought and prompt decision.

It is a well-known fact that the only manner in which an overpampered boy or girl may be made to become useful is by forcing him or her to become self-sustaining. This calls for the exercise of both imagination and decision, neither of which would be used except out of necessity.

July 24

From the very day that you reach a definite decision in your own mind as to the precise thing, condition, or position in life that you deeply desire, you will observe, if you read books, newspapers, and magazines, that important news items and other data bearing on the object of your Definite Chief Aim will begin to come to your attention; you will observe, also, that opportunities will begin to come to you that will, if embraced, lead you nearer and nearer the coveted goal of your desire. No one knows better than the author of this course how impossible and impractical this may seem to the person who is not informed on the subject of mind operation; however, this is not an age favorable to the doubter or the skeptic, and the best thing for any person to do is to experiment with this principle until its practicality has been established.

July 25

Procrastination robs you of opportunity. It is a significant fact that no great leader was ever known to procrastinate. You are fortunate if AMBITION drives you into action, never permitting you to falter or turn back once you have rendered a DECISION to go forward. Second by second, as the clock ticks off the distance, TIME is running a race with YOU. Delay means defeat, because no man may ever make up a second of lost TIME. TIME is a master worker which heals the wounds of failure and disappointment and rights all wrongs and turns all mistakes into capital, but it favors only those who kill off procrastination and remain in ACTION when decisions are to be made.

July 26

Ask any well-informed salesman and he will tell you that indecision is the outstanding weakness of the majority of people. Every salesman is familiar with that time-worn alibi, "I will think it over," which is the last trench-line of defense of those who have not the courage to say either yes or no.

The great leaders of the world were men and women of quick decision.

July 27

The suspense of indecision drives millions of people to failure. A condemned man once said that the thought of his approaching execution was not so terrifying, once he had reached the decision in his own mind to accept the inevitable.

July 28

The man of DECISION gets that which he goes after, no matter how long it takes or how difficult the task. An able salesman wanted to meet a Cleveland banker. The banker would not see him.

The man of DECISION cannot be stopped!

The man of INDECISION cannot be started! Take your own choice.

July 29

When Columbus began his famous voyage he made one of the most far-reaching DECISIONS in the history of mankind. Had he not remained firm on that decision, the freedom of America, as we know it today, would never have been known.

Take notice of those about you and observe this significant fact—THAT THE SUCCESSFUL MEN AND WOMEN ARE THOSE WHO REACH DECISIONS QUICKLY AND THEN STAND FIRMLY BY THOSE DECISIONS AFTER THEY ARE MADE.

July 30

If you are one of those who make up their minds today and change them again tomorrow, you are doomed to failure. If you are not sure which way to move, it is better to shut your eyes and move in the dark than to remain still and make no move at all.

The world will forgive you if you make mistakes, but it will never forgive you if you make no DECISIONS, because it will never hear of you outside of the community in which you live.

July 31

No matter who you are or what may be your life-work, you are playing checkers with TIME! It is always your next move. Move with quick DECISION and Time will favor you. Stand still and Time will wipe you off the board.

You cannot always make the right move, but if you make enough moves you may take advantage of the law of averages and pile up a creditable score before the great game of LIFE is ended.

August

The Eighth Step Toward Riches

PERSISTENCE

August 1

Persistence is an essential factor in the procedure of transmuting desire into its monetary equivalent. The basis of persistence is the power of will.

Willpower and desire, when properly combined, make an irresistible pair. Men who accumulate great fortunes are generally known as cold-blooded and, sometimes, ruthless. Often they are misunderstood. What they have is willpower, which they mix with persistence and place back of their desires to *ensure* the attainment of their objectives.

August 2

The majority of people are ready to throw their aims and purposes overboard, and give up at the first sign of opposition or misfortune. A few carry on despite all opposition until they attain their goal.

There may be no heroic connotation to the word *persistence*, but the quality is to the character of man what carbon is to steel.

August 3

The building of a fortune, generally, involves the application of the entire thirteen factors of this philosophy. These principles must be understood; they must be applied with persistence by all who accumulate money.

If you are following this book with the intention of applying the knowledge it conveys, your first test as to your persistence will come when you begin to follow the six steps described in the beginning (see page 6).

August 4

Lack of persistence is one of the major causes of failure. Moreover, experience with thousands of people has proved that lack of persistence is a weakness common to the majority of men. It is a weakness which may be overcome by effort. The ease with which lack of persistence may be conquered will depend *entirely* upon the intensity of one's desire.

August 5

The starting point of all achievement is desire. Keep this constantly in mind. Weak desires bring weak results, just as a small amount of fire makes a small amount of heat. If you find yourself lacking in persistence, this weakness may be remedied by building a stronger fire under your desires.

August 6

Fortunes gravitate to men whose minds have been prepared to "attract" them, just as surely as water gravitates to the ocean. In this book may be found all the stimuli necessary to "attune" any normal mind to the vibrations which will attract the object of one's desires.

If you find you are weak in persistence, surround yourself with a Master Mind group, and through the cooperative efforts of the members of this group, you can develop persistence.

August 7

Your subconscious mind works continuously while you are awake and while you are asleep.

Spasmodic, or occasional, effort to apply the rules will be of no value to you. To get results, you must apply all of the rules until their application becomes a fixed habit with you. In no other way can you develop the necessary "money consciousness."

Poverty is attracted to the one whose mind is favorable to it, as money is attracted to him whose mind has been deliberately prepared to attract it, and through the same laws. Poverty consciousness will voluntarily seize the mind which is not occupied with the money consciousness. A poverty consciousness develops without *conscious* application of habits favorable to it. The money consciousness must be created to order, unless one is born with such a consciousness.

August 8

Without persistence, you will be defeated even before you start. With persistence you will win.

You may find it necessary to "snap" out of your mental inertia, moving slowly at first, then increasing your speed, until you gain complete control over your will. Be persistent no matter how slowly you may, at first, have to move. With persistence will come success.

August 9

If you select your Master Mind group with care, you will have in it at least one person who will aid you in the development of persistence. Some who have accumulated great fortunes did so because of necessity. They developed the habit of persistence, because they were so closely driven by circumstances that they *had to become persistent.*

There is no substitute for persistence! It cannot be supplanted by any other quality! Remember this, and it will hearten you in the beginning, when the going may seem difficult and slow.

August 10

Those who have cultivated the habit of persistence seem to enjoy insurance against failure. No matter how many times they are defeated, they finally arrive up toward the top of the ladder. Sometimes it appears that there is a hidden Guide whose duty is to test men through all sorts of discouraging experiences. Those who pick themselves up after defeat and keep on trying arrive, and the world cries, "Bravo! I knew you could do it!" The hidden Guide lets no one enjoy great achievement without passing the persistence test. Those who can't take it simply do not make the grade.

Those who can "take it" are bountifully rewarded for their persistence. They receive, as their compensation, whatever goal they are pursuing. That is not all! They receive something infinitely more important than material compensation: the knowledge that "every failure brings with it the seed of an equivalent advantage."

August 11

A few people know from experience the soundness of persistence. They are the ones who have not accepted defeat as being anything more than temporary. They are the ones whose desires are so persistently applied that defeat is finally changed into victory. We who stand on the side-lines of Life see the overwhelmingly large number who go down in defeat, never to rise again. We see the few who take the punishment of defeat *as an urge to greater effort*. These, fortunately, never learn to accept Life's reverse gear. But what we do not see, what most of us never suspect of existing, is the silent but irresistible power which comes to the rescue of those who fight on in the face of discouragement. If we speak of this power at all we call it persistence and let it go at that. One thing we all know is that if one does not possess persistence, one does not achieve noteworthy success in any calling.

August 12

Persistence is a state of mind; therefore it can be cultivated. Like all states of mind, persistence is based upon definite causes, among them these:

a. *Definiteness of purpose.* Knowing what one wants is the first and most important step toward the development of persistence. A strong motive surmounts many difficulties.

b. *Desire.* It is easy to acquire and to maintain persistence in pursuing the object of intense desire.

c. *Self-reliance.* Belief in one's ability to carry out a plan encourages one to follow the plan through with persistence.

d. *Definiteness of plans.* Organized plans, even though they may be weak and entirely impractical, encourage persistence.

e. *Accurate knowledge.* Knowing that one's plans are sound, based upon experience or observation, encourages persistence; "guessing" instead of "knowing" destroys persistence.

f. *Cooperation*. Sympathy, understanding, and harmonious cooperation with others tend to develop persistence.

g. *Willpower*. The habit of concentrating one's thoughts upon the building of plans for the attainment of a definite purpose leads to persistence.

h. *Habit*. Persistence is the direct result of habit. Fear, the worst of all enemies, can be effectively cured *by forced repetition of acts of courage*.

August 13

Take inventory of yourself, and determine in what particular, if any, you are lacking in this essential quality of persistence. Measure yourself courageously, point by point, and see how many of the eight factors of persistence you lack. The analysis may lead to discoveries that will give you a new grip on yourself.

August 14

The weaknesses which must be mastered by all who accumulate riches include:

1. Failure to recognize and to clearly define exactly what one wants.
2. Procrastination. (Usually backed up with an alibi or excuse.)
3. Lack of interest in acquiring specialized knowledge.
4. Indecision
5. Relying upon alibis instead of creating definite plans for the solution of problems.
6. Self-satisfaction
7. Indifference
8. Blaming others for one's mistakes and accepting unfavorable circumstances as unavoidable.
9. Weakness of desire, due to neglect in the choice of motives that impel action.
10. Willingness to quit at the first sign of defeat. (Based upon the six basic fears.)

11. Lack of organized plans, placed in writing where they may be analyzed.

12. Neglecting to move on ideas or to grasp opportunity when it presents itself.

13. Wishing instead of willing.

14. Compromising with poverty instead of aiming at riches.

15. Searching for shortcuts to riches, trying to get without giving a fair equivalent, endeavoring to drive "sharp" bargains.

16. Fear of criticism, failure to create plans and to put them into action, because of what other people will think, do, or say.

August 15

Let us examine some of the symptoms of the Fear of Criticism. The majority of people permit relatives, friends, and the public at large to so influence them that they cannot live their own lives, because they fear criticism.

Huge numbers of people make mistakes in marriage, stand by the bargain, and go through life miserable and unhappy, because they fear criticism which may follow if they correct the mistake. Anyone who has submitted to this form of fear knows the irreparable damage it does, by destroying ambition, self-reliance, and the desire to achieve.

August 16

People refuse to take chances in business because they fear the criticism which may follow if they fail. *The fear of criticism in such cases is stronger than the desire for success.*

Too many people refuse to set high goals for themselves, or even neglect selecting a career, because they fear the criticism of relatives and "friends" who may say, "Don't aim so high; people will think you are crazy."

August 17

Many people believe that material success is the result of favorable "breaks." There is an element of ground for the belief, but those depending entirely upon luck are nearly always disappointed, because they overlook another important factor which must be present before one can be sure of success. It is the knowledge with which favorable "breaks" can be made to order.

The only "break" anyone can afford to rely upon is a self-made "break." These come through the application of persistence. The starting point is definiteness of purpose.

August 18

Examine the first hundred people you meet, ask them what they want most in life, and ninety-eight of them will not be able to tell you. If you press them for an answer, some will say security, many will say money, a few will say happiness, others will say fame and power, and still others will say social recognition, ease in living, ability to sing, dance, or write, but none of them will be able to define these terms or give the slightest indication of a plan by which they hope to attain these vaguely expressed wishes. Riches do not respond to wishes. They respond only to definite plans backed by definite desires through constant persistence.

August 19

There are four simple steps which lead to the habit of persistence. They call for no great amount of intelligence, no particular amount of education, and but little time or effort. The necessary steps are:

1. A definite purpose backed by burning desire for its fulfillment.
2. A definite plan expressed in continuous action.
3. A mind closed tightly against all negative and discouraging influences, including negative suggestions of relatives, friends, and acquaintances.
4. A friendly alliance with one or more persons who will encourage one to follow through with both plan and purpose.

These four steps are essential for success in all walks of life.

August 20

The entire purpose of the thirteen principles of this philosophy is to enable one to take these four steps (*see August 19*) as a matter of *habit*.

These are the steps by which one may control one's economic destiny.

They are the steps that lead to freedom and independence of thought.

They are the steps that lead to riches in small or great quantities.

They lead the way to power, fame, and worldly recognition.

They are the four steps which guarantee favorable "breaks."

They are the steps that convert dreams into physical realities.

They lead, also, to the mastery of fear, discouragement, indifference.

There is a magnificent reward for all who learn to take these four steps. It is the privilege of writing one's own ticket and of making Life yield whatever price is asked.

August 21

What mystical power gives to men of persistence the capacity to master difficulties? Does the quality of persistence set up in one's mind some form of spiritual, mental, or chemical activity which gives one access to supernatural forces? Does Infinite Intelligence throw *itself* on the side of the person who still fights on after the battle has been lost with the whole world on the opposing side?

These and many other similar questions have arisen in my mind as I have observed men like Henry Ford, who started at scratch and built an Industrial Empire of huge proportions with little else in the way of a beginning but persistence. Or Thomas A. Edison, who, with less than three months of schooling, became the world's leading inventor and converted persistence into the talking machine, the moving-picture machine, and the incandescent light, to say nothing of half a hundred other useful inventions.

I had the privilege of analyzing both Mr. Edison

and Mr. Ford over a long period of years, and therefore I speak from actual knowledge when I say that I found no quality, save persistence, in either of them, that even remotely suggested the major source of their stupendous achievements.

August 22

As one makes an impartial study of the prophets, philosophers, "miracle" men, and religious leaders of the past, one is drawn to the inevitable conclusion that persistence, concentration of effort, and definiteness of purpose were the major sources of their achievements.

August 23

One of the most common causes of failure is the habit of quitting when one is overtaken by *temporary defeat*. Every person is guilty of this mistake at one time or another.

More than five hundred of the most successful men this country has ever known told the author their greatest success came just one step *beyond* the point at which defeat had overtaken them.

Failure is a trickster with a keen sense of irony and cunning. It takes great delight in tripping one when success is almost within reach.

August 24

Bulldog determination, a persistence in standing back of a single desire, is destined to mow down all opposition and bring you the opportunity you seek.

The better portion of all sales that have been made were made after people had said "no."

August 25

Psychologists have correctly said that "when one is truly ready for a thing, it puts in its appearance." What a different story men would have to tell if only they would adopt a definite purpose and stand by that purpose until it had time to become an all-consuming obsession!

August 26

One of the main weaknesses of mankind is the average man's familiarity with the word *impossible*. He knows all the rules which will not work. He knows all the things which cannot be done. This book was written for those who seek the rules which have made others successful and are willing to *stake everything* on those rules.

August 27

We go through two important periods in this life: One is that period during which we are gathering, classifying, and organizing knowledge, and the other is that period during which we are struggling for recognition. We must first learn something, which requires more effort than most of us are willing to put into the job, but after we have learned much that can be of useful service to others, we are still confronted with the problem of convincing them that we can serve them.

One of the most important reasons why we should always be not only ready but willing to render service is the fact that every time we do so, we gain thereby another opportunity to prove to someone that we have ability; we go just one more step toward gaining the necessary recognition that we must all have.

Instead of saying to the world, "Show me the color of your money, and I will show you what I can do," reverse the rule and say, "Let me show you the color of my service so that I may take a look at the color of your money if you like my service."

August 28

The leader who successfully develops and directs the energies of a Master Mind must possess tact, patience, persistence, self-confidence, intimate knowledge of mind chemistry, and the ability to adapt himself (in a state of perfect poise and harmony) to quickly changing circumstances, without showing the least sign of annoyance.

August 29

Y ou now have within your possession the passkey to achievement. You have but to unlock the door to the Temple of Knowledge and walk in. But you must go to the Temple; it will not come to you. If these laws are new to you the "going" will not be easy at first. You will stumble many times, but keep moving! Very soon you will come to the brow of the mountain you have been climbing, and you will behold in the valleys below the rich estate of KNOWLEDGE, which shall be your reward for your faith and efforts.

Everything has a price. There is no such possibility as "something for nothing." In your experiments with the Law of the Master Mind you are jockeying with Nature in her highest and noblest form. Nature cannot be tricked or cheated. She will give up to you the object of your struggles only after you have paid her price, which is CONTINUOUS, UNYIELDING, PERSISTENT EFFORT!

August 30

You can get nowhere without persistence—a fact which cannot be too often repeated.

The difference between persistence and lack of it is the same as the difference between wishing for a thing and positively determining to get it.

To become a person of initiative you must form the habit of aggressively and persistently following the object of your definite chief aim until you acquire it, whether this requires one year or twenty years. You might as well have no Definite Chief Aim as to have such an aim without continuous effort to achieve it.

August 31

Take any person that you know who enjoys financial success, and he will tell you that he is being constantly sought and that opportunities to make money are constantly being urged upon him!

"To him that hath shall be given, but to him that hath not shall be taken away even that which he hath."

This quotation from the Bible used to seem ridiculous to me, yet how true it is when reduced to its concrete meaning.

Yes, "to him that hath shall be given!" If he "hath" failure, lack of self-confidence, hatred, or lack of self-control, to him shall these qualities be given in still greater abundance! But, if he "hath" success, self-confidence, self-control, patience, persistence, and determination, to him shall these qualities be increased!

SEPTEMBER

The Ninth Step Toward Riches

POWER OF THE
MASTER MIND

September 1

Power is essential for success in the accumulation of money. Plans are inert and useless without sufficient power to translate them into action. *Power* may be defined as "organized and intelligently directed knowledge." *Power,* as the term is here used, refers to organized effort sufficient to enable an individual to transmute desire into its monetary equivalent. Organized effort is produced through the coordination of effort of two or more people who work toward a definite end in a spirit of harmony.

September 2

Power is required for the accumulation of money! Power is necessary for the retention of money after it has been accumulated!

Let us ascertain how power may be acquired. If power is "organized knowledge," let us examine the sources of knowledge:

a. *Infinite Intelligence.* This source of knowledge may be contacted through the procedure described in another chapter, with the aid of Creative Imagination.

b. *Accumulated experience.* The accumulated experience of man (or that portion of it which has been organized and recorded) may be found in any well-equipped public library. An important part of this accumulated experience is taught in public schools and colleges, where it has been classified and organized.

c. *Experiment and research.* In the field of science, and in practically every other walk of life, men are gathering, classifying, and organizing new facts daily. This is the source to which one must turn when knowledge is not available through "accumulated experience." Here, too, the Creative Imagination must often be used.

September 3

Knowledge may be converted into power by organizing it into definite plans and by expressing those plans in terms of action.

September 4

Examination of the three major sources of knowledge (*see September 2*) will readily disclose the difficulty an individual would have, if he depended upon his efforts alone, in assembling knowledge and expressing it through definite plans in terms of action. If his plans are comprehensive and if they contemplate large proportions, he must, generally, induce others to cooperate with him before he can inject into them the necessary element of power.

September 5

The "Master Mind" may be defined as: "Coordination of knowledge and effort, in a spirit of harmony, between two or more people, for the attainment of a definite purpose."

No individual may have great power without availing himself of the Master Mind.

September 6

So you may better understand the "intangible" potentialities of power available to you through a properly chosen Master Mind group, we will here explain the two characteristics of the Master Mind principle, one of which is economic in nature and the other psychic. The economic feature is obvious. Economic advantages may be created by any person who surrounds himself with the advice, counsel, and personal cooperation of a group of men who are willing to lend him wholehearted aid in a spirit of perfect harmony. This form of cooperative alliance has been the basis of nearly every great fortune. Your understanding of this great truth may definitely determine your financial status.

The psychic phase of the Master Mind principle is much more abstract, much more difficult to comprehend, because it has reference to the spiritual forces with which the human race as a whole is not well acquainted. You may catch a significant suggestion from this statement: "No two minds ever come together without thereby creating a third, invisible, intangible force which may be likened to a third mind."

September 7

Keep in mind the fact that there are only two known elements in the whole universe: energy and matter. It is a well-known fact that matter may be broken down into units of molecules, atoms, and electrons. There are units of matter which may be isolated, separated, and analyzed.

Likewise, there are units of energy.

The human mind is a form of energy, a part of it being spiritual in nature. When the minds of two people are coordinated in a spirit of harmony, the spiritual units of energy of each mind form an affinity, which constitutes the "psychic" phase of the Master Mind.

September 8

Analyze the record of any man who has accumulated a great fortune and many of those who have accumulated modest fortunes, and you will find that they have either consciously or unconsciously employed the Master Mind principle.

Great power can be accumulated through no other principle!

September 9

Energy is Nature's universal set of building blocks, out of which she constructs every material thing in the universe, including man, and every form of animal and vegetable life. Through a process only Nature completely understands, she translates energy into matter.

Nature's building blocks are available to man in the energy involved in thinking! Man's brain may be compared to an electric battery: It absorbs energy from the ether, which permeates every atom of matter and fills the entire universe. It is a well-known fact that a group of electric batteries will provide more energy than a single battery. It is also a well-known fact that an individual battery will provide energy in proportion to the number and capacity of the cells it contains.

The brain functions in a similar fashion. This accounts for the fact that some brains are more efficient than others and leads to this significant statement: A group of brains coordinated (or connected) in a spirit of harmony will provide more thought energy than a single brain, just as a group of electric batteries will provide more energy than a single battery.

September 10

It becomes immediately obvious that the Master Mind principle holds the secret of the power wielded by men who surround themselves with other men of brains.

When a group of individual brains are coordinated and function in harmony, the increased energy created through that alliance becomes available to every individual brain in the group.

September 11

There is little if any doubt that Henry Ford was one of the best-informed men in the business and industrial world. The question of his wealth needs no discussion. Analyze Mr. Ford's intimate personal friends, and you will be prepared to understand the following statement: "Men take on the nature and the habits and the power of thought of those with whom they associate in a spirit of sympathy and harmony."

September 12

Henry Ford whipped poverty, illiteracy, and igno-rance by allying himself with great minds whose vibrations of thought he absorbed into his own mind. Through his association with Edison, Burbank, Burroughs, and Firestone, Mr. Ford added to his own brain power the sum and substance of the intelligence, experience, knowledge, and spiritual forces of these four men. Moreover, he appropriated and made use of the Master Mind principle through the methods of procedure described in this book.

This principle is available to you!

September 13

Mahatma Gandhi's power is passive, but it is real. His stupendous power may be explained in a few words. He came by power through inducing over two hundred million people to coordinate, with mind and body, in a spirit of harmony, for a definite purpose.

In brief, Gandhi accomplished a miracle, for it is a miracle when two hundred million people can be induced—not forced—to cooperate in a spirit of harmony for a limitless time. If you doubt that this is a miracle, try to induce any two people to cooperate in a spirit of harmony for *any length of time.*

September 14

Every man who manages a business knows what a difficult matter it is to get employees to work together in a spirit even remotely resembling harmony.

The list of the chief sources from which power may be attained is, as you have seen, headed by Infinite Intelligence. When two or more people coordinate in a spirit of harmony and work toward a definite objective they place themselves in position, through that alliance, to absorb power directly from the great universal storehouse of Infinite Intelligence. This is the greatest of all sources of power. It is the source to which the genius turns. It is the source to which every great leader turns (whether he may be conscious of the fact or not).

September 15

The other two major sources from which the knowledge necessary for the accumulation of power may be obtained are no more reliable than the five senses of man. The senses are not always reliable. Infinite Intelligence does not err.

September 16

Money is as shy and elusive as the "old-time" maiden. It must be wooed and won by methods not unlike those used by a determined lover in pursuit of the girl of his choice. And, coincidental as it is, the power used in the "wooing" of money is not greatly different from that used in wooing a maiden. That power, when successfully used in the pursuit of money, must be mixed with faith. It must be mixed with desire. It must be mixed with persistence. It must be applied through a plan, and that plan must be set into action.

September 17

When money comes in quantities known as "the big money," it flows to the one who accumulates it as easily as water flows downhill. There exists a great unseen stream of power, which may be compared to a river, except that one side flows in one direction, carrying all who get into that side of the stream onward and upward to wealth, and the other side flows in the opposite direction, carrying all who are unfortunate enough to get into it (and not able to extricate themselves from it) downward to misery and poverty.

September 18

Every man who has accumulated a great fortune has recognized the existence of this stream of life. It consists of one's thinking process. The positive emotions of thought form the side of the stream which carries one to fortune. The negative emotions form the side which carries one down to poverty.

If you are in the side of the stream of power which leads to poverty, this may serve as an oar, by which you may propel yourself over into the other side of the stream. It can serve you only through application and use. Merely reading and passing judgment on it, either one way or another, will in no way benefit you.

September 19

Some people undergo the experience of alternating between the positive and negative sides of the stream, being at times on the positive side and at times on the negative side. The Wall Street crash of '29 swept millions of people from the positive to the negative side of the stream. These millions are struggling, some of them in desperation and fear, to get back to the positive side of the stream. This book was written especially for those millions.

September 20

Poverty and riches often change places. The Crash taught the world this truth, although the world will not long remember the lesson. Poverty may, and generally does, voluntarily take the place of riches. When riches take the place of poverty, the change is usually brought about through well-conceived and carefully executed PLANS. Poverty needs no plan. It needs no one to aid it, because it is bold and ruthless. Riches are shy and timid. They have to be "attracted."

Anybody can wish for riches, and most people do, but only a few know that a definite plan plus a burning desire for wealth are the only dependable means of accumulating wealth.

September 21

The Master Mind means a mind that is developed through the harmonious cooperation of two or more people who ally themselves for the purpose of accomplishing any given task.

If you are engaged in the business of selling you may profitably experiment with this Law of the Master Mind in your daily work. It has been found that a group of six or seven salespeople may use the law so effectively that their sales may be increased to unbelievable proportions.

September 22

When two or more people harmonize their minds and produce the effect known as a Master Mind, each person in the group becomes vested with the power to contact with and gather knowledge through the "subconscious" minds of all the other members of the group. This power becomes immediately noticeable, having the effect of stimulating the mind to a higher rate of vibration and otherwise evidencing itself in the form of a more vivid imagination and the consciousness of what appears to be a sixth sense. It is through this sixth sense that new ideas will "flash" into the mind. These ideas take on the nature and form of the subject dominating the mind of the individual. If the entire group has met for the purpose of discussing a given subject, ideas concerning that subject will come pouring into the minds of all present, as if an outside influence were dictating them. The minds of those participating in the Master Mind become as magnets, attracting ideas and thought stimuli of the most highly organized and practical nature from—no one knows where!

September 23

The process of mind-blending described as a Master Mind, may be likened to the act of one who connects many electric batteries to a single transmission wire, thereby "stepping up" the power flowing over that line. Each battery added increases the power passing over that line by the amount of energy the battery carries. Just so in the case of blending individual minds into a Master Mind. Each mind, through the principle of mind chemistry, stimulates all the other minds in the group, until the mind energy thus becomes so great that it penetrates to and connects with the universal energy known as ether, which, in turn, touches every atom of the entire universe.

September 24

You can do it if you believe you can! You have failed many times? How fortunate! You ought to know by now some of the things NOT to do.

September 25

Many millions of people believe themselves to possess WISDOM. Many of these do possess wisdom in certain elementary stages, but no man may possess real wisdom without the aid of the power known as a Master Mind, and such a mind cannot be created except through the blending, in harmony, of two or more minds.

Without the blending and harmonizing of two or more minds (twelve or thirteen minds appear to be the most favorable number) may be produced a mind which has the capacity to "tune in" on the vibrations of the ether and pick up from that source kindred thoughts on any subject.

September 26

All the so-called geniuses probably gained their reputations because, by mere chance or otherwise, they formed alliances with other minds which enabled them to "step up" their own mind vibrations to where they were enabled to contact the vast Temple of Knowledge recorded and filed in the ether of the universe.

September 27

Search where you will, wherever you find an outstanding success in business, finance, industry or in any of the professions, you may be sure that back of the success is some individual who has applied the principle of mind chemistry, out of which a Master Mind has been created. These outstanding successes often appear to be the handiwork of but one person, but search closely and the other individuals whose minds have been coordinated with his own may be found.

Remember that two or more persons may operate the principle of mind chemistry so as to create a Master Mind.

September 28

POWER (manpower) is ORGANIZED KNOWL-EDGE EXPRESSED THROUGH INTELLI-GENT EFFORTS!

No effort can be said to be ORGANIZED unless the individuals engaged in the effort coordinate their knowledge and energy in a spirit of perfect harmony. Lack of such harmonious coordination of effort is the main cause of practically every business failure.

September 29

One may hardly glance at the news of a day's events without seeing a report of some business, industrial, or financial merger, bringing under one management enormous resources and thus creating great power.

One day it is a group of banks; another day it is a chain of railroads; the next day it is a combination of steel plants, all merging for the purpose of developing power through highly organized and coordinated effort.

Knowledge, general in nature and unorganized, is not POWER; it is only potential power—the material out of which real power may be developed.

September 30

It must not be assumed that a Master Mind will imme-diately spring, mushroom fashion, out of every group of minds which make pretense of coordination in a spirit of HARMONY!

Harmony is the nucleus around which the state of mind known as Master Mind must be developed. With-out this element of harmony there can be no Master Mind—a truth which cannot be repeated too often.

OCTOBER

The Tenth Step Toward Riches

THE MYSTERY OF SEX TRANSMUTATION

October 1

The meaning of the word *transmute* is, in simple language, "the changing, or transferring of one element, or form of energy, into another."

The emotion of sex brings into being a state of mind. Because of ignorance on the subject, this state of mind is generally associated with the physical, and because of improper influences, to which most people have been subjected, in acquiring knowledge of sex, things essentially physical have highly biased the mind.

The emotion of sex has back of it the possibility of three constructive potentialities; they are:

1. The perpetuation of mankind.
2. The maintenance of health (as a therapeutic agency, it has no equal).
3. The transformation of mediocrity into genius through transmutation.

October 2

Sex transmutation is simple and easily explained. It means the switching of the mind from thoughts of physical expression to thoughts of some other nature.

Sex desire is the most powerful of human desires. When driven by this desire, men develop keenness of imagination, courage, willpower, persistence, and creative ability unknown to them at other times.

October 3

So strong and impelling is the desire for sexual contact that men freely run the risk of life and reputation to indulge it. When harnessed and redirected along other lines, this motivating force maintains all of its attributes of keenness of imagination, courage, etc., which may be used as powerful creative forces in literature, art, or any other profession or calling, including, of course, the accumulation of riches.

October 4

The transmutation of sex energy calls for the exercise of willpower to be sure, but the reward is worth the effort. The desire for sexual expression is inborn and natural. The desire cannot and should not be submerged or eliminated. But it should be given an outlet through forms of expression which enrich the body, mind, and spirit of man. If not given this form of outlet, through transmutation, it will seek outlets through purely physical channels.

October 5

A river may be dammed and its water controlled for a time, but eventually it will force an outlet. The same is true of the emotion of sex. It may be submerged and controlled for a time, but its very nature causes it to be ever seeking means of expression. If it is not transmuted into some creative effort it will find a less worthy outlet.

Fortunate, indeed, is the person who has discovered how to give sex emotion an outlet through some form of creative effort, for he has, by that discovery, lifted himself to the status of a genius.

October 6

Scientific research has disclosed these significant facts:

1. The men of greatest achievement are men with highly developed sex natures—men who have learned the art of sex transmutation.

2. The men who have accumulated great fortunes and achieved outstanding recognition in literature, art, industry, architecture, and the professions, were motivated by the influence of a woman.

The research from which these astounding discoveries were made went back through the pages of biography and history for more than two thousand years. Wherever there was evidence available in connection with the lives of men and women of great achievement, it indicated most convincingly that they possessed highly developed sex natures.

October 7

The emotion of sex is an "irresistible force" against which there can be no such opposition as an "immovable body." When driven by this emotion, men become gifted with a super power for action. Understand this truth, and you will catch the significance of the statement that sex transmutation will lift one to the status of a genius.

October 8

The emotion of sex contains the secret of creative ability. Destroy the sex glands, whether in man or beast, and you have removed the major source of action. For proof of this, observe what happens to any animal after it has been castrated. A bull becomes as docile as a cow after it has been altered sexually. Sex alteration takes out of the male, whether man or beast, all the fight that was in him. Sex alteration of the female has the same effect.

October 9

The human mind responds to stimuli through which it may be "keyed up" to high rates of vibration, known as enthusiasm, creative imagination, intense desire, etc. The stimuli to which the mind responds most freely are:

1. The desire for sex expression
2. Love
3. A burning desire for fame, power, or financial gain, money
4. Music
5. Friendship between either those of the same sex or those of the opposite sex
6. A Master Mind alliance based upon the harmony of two or more people who ally themselves for spiritual or temporal advancement
7. Mutual suffering, such as that experienced by people who are persecuted
8. Auto-suggestion
9. Fear
10. Narcotics and alcohol

October 10

The desire for sex expression comes at the head of the list of stimuli, which most effectively "step up" the vibrations of the mind and start the "wheels" of physical action. Eight of these stimuli (*see list on October 9*) are natural and constructive. Two are destructive. The list is here presented for the purpose of enabling you to make a comparative study of the major sources of mind stimulation. From this study, it will be readily seen that the emotion of sex is, by great odds, the most intense and powerful of all mind stimuli.

This comparison is necessary as a foundation for proof of the statement that transmutation of sex energy may lift one to the status of a genius.

October 11

Let us find out what constitutes a genius.

Some wiseacre has said that a genius is a man who "wears long hair, eats queer food, lives alone, and serves as a target for the joke makers." A better definition of a genius is "a man who has discovered how to increase the vibrations of thought to the point where he can freely communicate with sources of knowledge not available through the ordinary rate of vibration of thought."

October 12

The salesman who knows how to take his mind off the subject of sex and direct it in sales effort with as much enthusiasm and determination as he would apply to its original purpose, has acquired the art of sex transmutation—whether he knows it or not. The majority of salesmen who transmute their sex energy do so without being in the least aware of what they are doing or how they are doing it.

October 13

G enius" is developed through the sixth sense. The reality of a sixth sense has been fairly well established. This sixth sense is Creative Imagination. The faculty of creative imagination is one which the majority of people never use during an entire lifetime, and if used at all it usually happens by mere accident. A relatively small number of people use, with deliberation and purpose aforethought, the faculty of creative imagination. Those who use this faculty voluntarily and with understanding of its functions are genii.

October 14

The faculty of creative imagination is the direct link between the finite mind of man and Infinite Intelligence. All so-called revelations referred to in the realm of religion and all discoveries of basic or new principles in the field of invention take place through the faculty of creative imagination.

October 15

When ideas or concepts flash into one's mind, through what is popularly called a "hunch," they come from one or more of the following sources:

1. Infinite Intelligence
2. One's subconscious mind, wherein is stored every sense impression and thought impulse which ever reached the brain through any of the five senses
3. From the mind of some other person who has just released the thought, or picture of the idea or concept, through conscious thought, or
4. From the other person's subconscious storehouse.

There are no other known sources from which inspired ideas, or hunches, may be received.

October 16

The creative imagination functions best when the mind is vibrating (due to some form of mind stimulation) at an exceedingly high rate. That is, when the mind is functioning at a rate of vibration higher than that of ordinary, normal thought.

When brain action has been stimulated, through one or more of the ten mind stimulants, it has the effect of lifting the individual far above the horizon of ordinary thought, and permits him to envision distance, scope, and quality of thoughts not available on the lower plane, such as that occupied while one is engaged in the solution of the problems of business and professional routine.

October 17

When lifted to this higher level of thought, through any form of mind stimulation, an individual occupies, relatively, the same position as one who has ascended in an airplane to a height from which he may see over and beyond the horizon line which limits his vision, while on the ground. Moreover, while on this higher level of thought, the individual is not hampered or bound by any of the stimuli which circumscribe and limit his vision while wrestling with the problems of gaining the three basic necessities of food, clothing, and shelter. He is in a world of thought in which the ordinary, workaday thoughts have been as effectively removed as are the hills and valleys and other limitations of physical vision when he rises in an airplane.

October 18

While on this exalted plane of thought, the creative faculty of the mind is given freedom for action. The way has been cleared for the sixth sense to function; it becomes receptive to ideas which could not reach the individual under any other circumstances. The sixth sense is the faculty which marks the difference between a genius and an ordinary individual.

The creative faculty becomes more alert and receptive to vibrations originating outside the individual's subconscious mind the more this faculty is used and the more the individual relies upon it and makes demands upon it for thought impulses. This faculty can be cultivated and developed only through use.

October 19

That which is known as one's "conscience" operates entirely through the faculty of the sixth sense.

The great artists, writers, musicians, and poets become great, because they acquire the habit of relying upon the "still small voice" which speaks from within, through the faculty of creative imagination. It is a fact well known to people who have "keen" imaginations that their best ideas come through so-called hunches.

October 20

There is a great orator who does not attain to greatness until he closes his eyes and begins to rely entirely upon the faculty of Creative Imagination. When asked why he closed his eyes just before the climaxes of his oratory, he replied, "I do it, because then I speak through ideas which come to me from within."

One of America's most successful and best-known financiers followed the habit of closing his eyes for two or three minutes before making a decision. When asked why he did this, he replied, "With my eyes closed, I am able to draw upon a source of superior intelligence."

October 21

Dr. Elmer R. Gates created more than two hundred useful patents through the process of cultivating and using the creative faculty. His method is both significant and interesting to one interested in attaining to the status of genius.

In his laboratory, he had what he called his "personal communication room." It was equipped with a small table on which he kept a pad of writing paper. When Dr. Gates desired to draw upon the forces available to him through his Creative Imagination, he would go into this room, seat himself at the table, shut off the lights, and concentrate upon the known factors of the invention on which he was working, remaining in that position until ideas began to "flash" into his mind in connection with the unknown factors of the invention.

On one occasion, ideas came through so fast that he was forced to write for almost three hours. When the thoughts stopped flowing and he examined his notes, he found they contained a minute description of principles which had no parallel among the known data of the scientific world. Moreover, the answer to his problem was intelligently presented in those notes. In this manner Dr. Gates completed over two hundred patents.

October 22

The reasoning faculty is often faulty, because it is largely guided by one's accumulated experience. Not all knowledge which one accumulates through "experience" is accurate. Ideas received through the creative faculty are much more reliable, for the reason that they come from sources more reliable than any which are available to the reasoning faculty of the mind.

The major difference between the genius and the ordinary "crank" inventor may be found in the fact that the genius works through his faculty of creative imagination, while the "crank" knows nothing of this faculty. The scientific inventor makes use of both the synthetic and the creative faculties of imagination.

October 23

The scientific inventor, or genius, begins an invention by organizing and combining the known ideas, or principles accumulated through experience, through the synthetic faculty (the reasoning faculty). If he finds this accumulated knowledge to be insufficient for the completion of his invention, he then draws upon the sources of knowledge available to him through his *creative* faculty. The method by which he does this varies with the individual, but this is the sum and substance of his procedure:

1. He stimulates his mind so that it vibrates on a higher-than-average plane by using one or more of the ten mind stimulants or some other stimulant of his choice.

2. He concentrates upon the known factors (the finished part) of his invention, and creates in his mind a perfect picture of unknown factors (the unfinished part) of his invention. He holds this picture in mind until it has been taken over by the subconscious mind,

then relaxes by clearing his mind of all thought and waits for his answer to "flash" into his mind.

Sometimes the results are both definite and immediate. At other times, the results are negative, depending upon the state of development of the "sixth sense," or creative faculty.

October 24

There is plenty of reliable evidence that the faculty of creative imagination exists. This evidence is available through accurate analysis of men who have become leaders in their respective callings without having had extensive educations. Lincoln was a notable example of a great leader who achieved greatness through the discovery and use of his faculty of creative imagination. He discovered and began to use this faculty as the result of the stimulation of love which he experienced after he met Anne Rutledge—a statement of the highest significance in connection with the study of the source of genius.

October 25

Intemperance in sex habits is just as detrimental as intemperance in habits of drinking and eating. In this age in which we live, an age which began with the world war, intemperance in habits of sex is common. This orgy of indulgence may account for the shortage of great leaders. No man can avail himself of the forces of his creative imagination while dissipating them. Man is the only creature on earth which violates Nature's purpose in this connection. Every other animal indulges its sex nature in moderation and with purpose which harmonizes with the laws of Nature. Every other animal responds to the call of sex only in "season." Man's inclination is to declare "open season."

Every intelligent person knows that stimulation in excess through alcoholic drink and narcotics is a form of intemperance which destroys the vital organs of the body, including the brain. Not every person knows, however, that overindulgence in sex expression may become a habit as destructive and as detrimental to creative effort as narcotics or liquor.

October 26

The human mind responds to stimulation! Among the greatest and most powerful of these stimuli is the urge of sex. When harnessed and transmuted, this driving force is capable of lifting men into that higher sphere of thought which enables them to master the sources of worry and petty annoyance which beset their pathway on the lower plane.

Unfortunately, only the genii have made the discovery. Others have accepted the experience of sex urge without discovering one of its major potentialities—a fact which accounts for the great number of "others" as compared to the limited number of genii.

October 27

The road to genius consists of the development, control, and use of sex, love, and romance. Briefly, the process may be stated as follows:

Encourage the presence of these emotions as the dominating thoughts in one's mind, and discourage the presence of all the destructive emotions. The mind is a creature of habit. It thrives upon the *dominating* thoughts fed it. Through the faculty of willpower, one may discourage the presence of any emotion and encourage the presence of any other. Control of the mind through the power of will is not difficult. Control comes from persistence and habit. The secret of control lies in understanding the process of transmutation. When any negative emotion presents itself in one's mind, it can be transmuted into a positive, or constructive, emotion by the simple procedure of changing one's thoughts.

October 28

Sex energy is the creative energy of all genii. *There never has been and never will be a great leader, builder, or artist lacking in this driving force of sex.*

Surely no one will misunderstand these statements to mean that all who are highly sexed are genii! Man attains to the status of a genius only when, and if, he stimulates his mind so that it draws upon the forces available, through the creative faculty of the imagination. Chief among the stimuli with which this "stepping up" of the vibrations may be produced is sex energy. The mere *possession of* this energy is not sufficient to produce a genius. The energy must be *transmuted* from desire for physical contact, into some other form of desire and action, before it will lift one to the status of a genius.

Far from becoming genii, because of great sex desires, the majority of men *lower* themselves, through misunderstanding and misuse of this great force, to the status of the lower animals.

October 29

Men seldom succeed before forty. I discovered, from the analysis of over 25,000 people, that men who succeed in an outstanding way, seldom do so before the age of forty, and more often they do not strike their real pace until they are well beyond the age of fifty. This fact was so astounding that it prompted me to go into the study of its cause most carefully, carrying the investigation over a period of more than twelve years.

This study disclosed the fact that the major reason why the majority of men who succeed do not begin to do so before the ages of forty to fifty is their tendency to dissipate their energies through overindulgence in physical expression of the emotion of sex. The majority of men *never* learn that the urge of sex has other possibilities, which far transcend in importance that of mere physical expression. The majority of those who make this discovery, do so *after having wasted many years* at a period when the sex energy is at its height, prior to the age of forty-five to fifty. This usually is followed by noteworthy achievement.

The lives of many men up to, and sometimes well

past, the age of forty, reflect a continued dissipation of energies which could have been more profitably turned into better channels. Their finer and more powerful emotions are sown wildly to the four winds. Out of this habit of the male grew the term "sowing his wild oats."

October 30

The desire for sexual expression is by far the strongest and most impelling of all the human emotions, and for this very reason this desire, when *harnessed and transmuted* into action other than that of physical expression, may raise one to the status of a genius.

Nature has prepared her own potions with which men may safely stimulate their minds so they vibrate on a plane that enables them to tune in to fine and rare thoughts which come from—no man knows where! No satisfactory substitute for Nature's stimulants has ever been found.

The world is ruled and the destiny of civilization is established by the human emotions. People are influenced in their actions not by reason so much as by "feelings." The creative faculty of the mind is set into action entirely by emotions and *not by cold reason*. The most powerful of all human emotions is that of sex. There are other mind stimulants, some of which have been listed, but no one of them or all of them combined can equal the driving power of sex.

October 31

There is no other road to genius than through voluntary self-effort! A man may attain to great heights of financial or business achievement, solely by the driving force of sex energy, but history is filled with evidence that he may, and usually does, carry with him certain traits of character which rob him of the ability to either hold or enjoy his fortune.

The emotion of love brings out and develops the artistic and the aesthetic nature of man. It leaves its impress upon one's very soul, even after the fire has been subdued by time and circumstance.

Love is, without question, life's greatest experience. It brings one into communion with Infinite Intelligence. When mixed with the emotions of romance and sex, it may lead one far up the ladder of creative effort. The emotions of love, sex, and romance are sides of the eternal triangle of achievement-building genius. Nature creates genii through no other force.

NOVEMBER

*The Eleventh and Twelfth Steps
Toward Riches*

THE SUBCONSCIOUS MIND /
THE BRAIN

November 1

The subconscious mind consists of a field of consciousness in which every impulse of thought that reaches the objective mind through any of the five senses is classified and recorded, and from which thoughts may be recalled or withdrawn as letters may be taken from a filing cabinet. It receives, and files, sense impressions or thoughts, regardless of their nature. You may voluntarily plant in your subconscious mind any plan, thought, or purpose which you desire to translate into its physical or monetary equivalent.

November 2

The subconscious acts first on the dominating desires which have been mixed with emotional feeling, such as faith. The subconscious mind works day and night. Through a method of procedure unknown to man, the subconscious mind draws upon the forces of Infinite Intelligence for the power with which it voluntarily transmutes one's desires into their physical equivalent, making use always of the most practical media by which this end may be accomplished.

November 3

You cannot *entirely* control your subconscious mind, but you can voluntarily hand over to it any plan, desire, or purpose which you wish transformed into concrete form. There is plenty of evidence to support the belief that the subconscious mind is the connecting link between the finite mind of man and Infinite Intelligence. It is the intermediary through which one may draw upon the forces of Infinite Intelligence at will. It, alone, contains the secret process by which mental impulses are modified and changed into their spiritual equivalent. It, alone, is the medium through which prayer may be transmitted to the source capable of answering prayer.

November 4

The possibilities of creative effort connected with the subconscious mind are stupendous and imponderable. They inspire one with awe.

I never approach the discussion of the subconscious mind without a feeling of littleness and inferiority due, perhaps, to the fact that man's entire stock of knowledge on this subject is so pitifully limited. The very fact that the subconscious mind is the medium of communication between the thinking mind of man and Infinite Intelligence is, of itself, a thought which almost paralyzes one's reason.

November 5

After you have accepted, as a reality, the existence of the subconscious mind and understand its possibilities as a medium for transmuting your desires into their physical or monetary equivalent, you will comprehend the full significance of the instructions of the six steps at the beginning of this book (see page 6). You will also understand why you have been repeatedly admonished to make your desires clear and to reduce them to writing. You will also understand the necessity of persistence in carrying out instructions.

The thirteen principles are the stimuli with which you acquire the ability to reach and to influence your subconscious mind. Do not become discouraged if you cannot do this upon the first attempt. Remember that the subconscious mind may be voluntarily directed *only through habit*. You have not yet had time to master faith. Be patient. Be persistent.

November 6

Remember, your subconscious mind functions voluntarily, *whether you make any effort to influence it or not*. This, naturally, suggests to you that thoughts of fear and poverty and all negative thoughts serve as stimuli to your subconscious mind, *unless* you master these impulses and give it more desirable food upon which it may feed.

November 7

The subconscious mind will not remain idle! If you fail to plant desires in your subconscious mind, it will feed upon the thoughts which reach it *as the result of your neglect*. We have already explained that thought impulses, both negative and positive, are reaching the subconscious mind continuously.

Remember that you are living *daily* in the midst of all manner of thought impulses, which are reaching your subconscious mind without your knowledge. Some of these impulses are negative; some are positive. You are now engaged in trying to help shut off the flow of negative impulses and to aid in voluntarily influencing your subconscious mind through positive impulses of desire. When you achieve this, you will possess the key which unlocks the door to your subconscious mind, and you will control that door so completely that no undesirable thought may influence your subconscious mind.

November 8

Everything which man creates begins in the form of a thought impulse. Man can create nothing which he does not first conceive in thought. Through the aid of the imagination, thought impulses may be assembled into plans. The imagination, when under control, may be used for the creation of plans or purposes that lead to success in one's chosen occupation.

November 9

All thought impulses intended for transmutation into their physical equivalent voluntarily planted in the subconscious mind must pass through the imagination and be mixed with faith. The "mixing" of faith with a plan, or purpose, intended for submission to the subconscious mind may be done only through the imagination. You will readily observe that voluntary use of the subconscious mind calls for coordination and application of all the principles.

November 10

Ella Wheeler Wilcox gave evidence of her under-standing of the power of the subconscious mind when she wrote:

> You never can tell what a thought will do
>   In bringing you hate or love—
> For thoughts are things, and their airy wings
>   Are swifter than carrier doves.
> They follow the law of the universe—
>   Each thing creates its kind,
> And they speed O'er the track to bring you back
>   Whatever went out from your mind.

Mrs. Wilcox understood the truth that thoughts which go out from one's mind, also imbed themselves deeply in one's subconscious mind, where they serve as a magnet, pattern, or blueprint by which the subconscious mind is influenced while translating them into their physical equivalent. Thoughts are truly things, for the reason that every material thing begins in the form of thought energy.

November 11

The subconscious mind is more susceptible to influence by impulses of thought mixed with "feeling" or emotion than by those originating solely in the reasoning portion of the mind. In fact, there is much evidence to support the theory that only emotionalized thoughts have any action influence upon the subconscious mind. It is a well-known fact that emotion or feeling rules the majority of people. If it is true that the subconscious mind responds more quickly to, and is influenced more readily by, thought impulses which are well mixed with emotion, it is essential to become familiar with the more important of the emotions.

November 12

Negative emotions *voluntarily* inject themselves into the thought impulses, which ensure passage into the subconscious mind. Positive emotions must be injected, through the principle of auto-suggestion, into the thought impulses which an individual wishes to pass on to his subconscious mind.

These emotions, or feeling impulses, constitute the action element, which transforms thought impulses from the passive to the active state. Thus may one understand why thought impulses which have been well mixed with emotion are acted upon more readily than thought impulses originating in "cold reason."

November 13

You are preparing yourself to influence and control the "inner audience" of your subconscious mind in order to hand over to it the desire for money, which you wish transmuted into its monetary equivalent. It is essential, therefore, that you understand the method of approach to this "inner audience." You must speak its language, or it will not heed your call. It understands best the language of emotion or feeling.

November 14

THE SEVEN MAJOR POSITIVE EMOTIONS

The emotion of desire
The emotion of faith
The emotion of love
The emotion of sex
The emotion of enthusiasm
The emotion of romance
The emotion of hope

There are other positive emotions, but these are the seven most powerful and the ones most commonly used in creative effort. Master these seven emotions (they can be mastered only by use), and the other positive emotions will be at your command when you need them. Remember, in this connection, that you are studying a book which is intended to help you develop a "money consciousness" *by filling your mind with positive emotions.*

November 15

THE SEVEN MAJOR NEGATIVE EMOTIONS
(to be avoided)

The emotion of fear
The emotion of jealousy
The emotion of hatred
The emotion of revenge
The emotion of greed
The emotion of superstition
The emotion of anger

Positive and negative emotions cannot occupy the mind at the same time. One or the other must dominate. One does not become money conscious by filling one's mind with negative emotions.

November 16

It is your responsibility to make sure that positive emotions constitute the dominating influence of your mind. Here the law of habit will come to your aid. *Form the habit* of applying and using the positive emotions! Eventually, they will dominate your mind so completely that the negatives *cannot enter it*.

November 17

The presence of a single negative in your conscious mind is sufficient to *destroy* all chances of constructive aid from your subconscious mind.

If you are an observing person, you must have noticed that most people resort to prayer only after everything else has failed! Or else they pray by a ritual of meaningless words. And because it is a fact that most people who pray do so only after everything else has failed, they go to prayer with their minds filled with fear and doubt, *which are the emotions the subconscious mind acts upon,* and passes on to Infinite Intelligence. Likewise, that is the emotion which Infinite Intelligence receives, and acts upon. If you pray for a thing, but have fear as you pray that you may not receive it or that your prayer will not be acted upon by Infinite Intelligence, your prayer *will have been in vain.*

November 18

Prayer does, sometimes, result in the realization of that for which one prays. If you have ever had the experience of receiving that for which you prayed, go back in your memory, and recall your actual state of mind while you were praying, and you will know, for sure, that the theory here described is more than a theory.

November 19

The time will come when the schools and educational institutions of the country will teach the "science of prayer." Moreover, then prayer may and will be reduced to a science. When that time comes, no one will approach the Universal Mind in a state of fear, for the very good reason that there will be no such emotion as fear. Ignorance, superstition, and false teaching will have disappeared, and man will have attained his true status as a child of Infinite Intelligence. A few have already attained this blessing.

If you believe this prophecy is far-fetched, take a look at the human race in retrospect. Less than a hundred years ago, men believed lightning to be evidence of the wrath of God and feared it. Now, thanks to the power of faith, men have harnessed lightning and made it turn the wheels of industry.

November 20

There are no tollgates between the finite mind of man and Infinite Intelligence. The communication costs nothing except Patience, Faith, Persistence, Understanding, and a sincere desire to communicate. Moreover, the approach can be made only by the individual himself. Paid prayers are worthless. Infinite Intelligence does no business by proxy. You either go direct, or you do not communicate.

You may buy prayer books and repeat them until the day of your doom without avail. Thoughts which you wish to communicate to Infinite Intelligence must undergo transformation, such as can be given only through your own subconscious mind.

November 21

The method by which you may communicate with Infinite Intelligence is very similar to that through which the vibration of sound is communicated by radio. If you understand the working principle of radio, you, of course, know that sound cannot be communicated through the ether until it has been "stepped up," or changed into a rate of vibration which the human ear cannot detect. The radio sending station picks up the sound of the human voice and "scrambles," or modifies, it by stepping up the vibration millions of times. Only in this way can the vibration of sound be communicated through the ether. After this transformation has taken place, the ether "picks up" the energy (which originally was in the form of vibrations of sound), carries that energy to radio receiving stations, and these receiving sets "step" that energy back down to its original rate of vibration so it is recognized as sound.

November 22

The subconscious mind is the intermediary which translates one's prayers into terms which Infinite Intelligence can recognize, presents the message, and brings back the answer in the form of a definite plan or idea for procuring the object of the prayer. Understand this principle, and you will know why mere words read from a prayer book cannot, and will never, serve as an agency of communication between the mind of man and Infinite Intelligence.

Before your prayer will reach Infinite Intelligence (a statement of the author's theory only), it probably is transformed from its original thought vibration into terms of spiritual vibration. Faith is the only known agency which will give your thoughts a spiritual nature. Faith and fear make poor bedfellows. *Where one is found, the other cannot exist.*

November 23

More than twenty years ago, the author, working in conjunction with the late Dr. Alexander Graham Bell and Dr. Elmer R. Gates observed that every human brain is both a broadcasting and receiving station for the vibration of thought.

Through the medium of the ether, in a fashion similar to that employed by the radio broadcasting principle, every human brain is capable of picking up vibrations of thought which are being released by other brains.

November 24

In connection with the statement of the preceding day, compare and consider the description of the Creative Imagination. The Creative Imagination is the "receiving set" of the brain, which receives thoughts released by the brains of others. It is the agency of communication between one's conscious, or reasoning, mind and the four sources from which one may receive thought stimuli.

November 25

When stimulated, or "stepped up," to a high rate of vibration, the mind becomes more receptive to the vibration of thought which reaches it through the ether from outside sources. This "stepping-up" process takes place through the positive emotions or the negative emotions. Through the emotions, the vibrations of thought may be increased. Vibrations of an exceedingly high rate are the only vibrations picked up and carried by the ether from one brain to another. Thought is energy traveling at an exceedingly high rate of vibration. Thought, which has been modified or "stepped up" by any of the major emotions, vibrates at a much higher rate than ordinary thought, and it is this type of thought which passes from one brain to another through the broadcasting machinery of the human brain.

November 26

The emotion of sex stands at the head of the list of human emotions as far as intensity and driving force are concerned. The brain which has been stimulated by the emotion of sex vibrates at a much more rapid rate than it does when that emotion is quiescent or absent. The result of sex transmutation is the increase of the rate of vibration of thoughts to such a pitch that the Creative Imagination becomes highly receptive to ideas, which it picks up from the ether. On the other hand, when the brain is vibrating at a rapid rate, it not only attracts thoughts and ideas released by other brains through the medium of the ether, but it gives to one's own thoughts that "feeling" which is essential before those thoughts will be picked up and acted upon by one's subconscious mind. Thus, you will see that the broadcasting principle is the factor through which you mix feeling, or emotion, with your thoughts and pass them on to your subconscious mind.

November 27

The subconscious mind is the "sending station" of the brain, through which vibrations of thought are broadcast. The Creative Imagination is the "receiving set," through which the vibrations of thought are picked up from the ether.

Along with the important factors of the subconscious mind and the faculty of the Creative Imagination, which constitute the sending and receiving sets of your mental broadcasting machinery, consider now the principle of auto-suggestion, which is the medium by which you may put into operation your "broadcasting" station.

Operation of your mental "broadcasting" station is a comparatively simple procedure. You have but three principles to bear in mind and to apply when you wish to use your broadcasting station: the subconscious mind, creative imagination, and auto-suggestion.

November 28

Great forces are "intangible." Through the ages which have passed, man has depended too much upon his physical senses and has limited his knowledge to physical things, which he could see, touch, weigh, and measure.

We are now entering the most marvelous of all ages, an age which will teach us something of the intangible forces of the world about us. Perhaps we shall learn, as we pass through this age, that the "other self" is more powerful than the physical self we see when we look into a mirror.

Sometimes men speak lightly of the intangibles— the things they cannot perceive through any of their five senses—and when we hear them, it should remind us that *all of us are controlled by forces which are unseen and intangible.*

November 29

The whole of mankind has not the power to cope with or control the intangible force wrapped up in the rolling waves of the oceans. Man has not the capacity to understand the intangible force of gravity, which keeps this little earth suspended midair and keeps man from falling from it, much less the power to control that force. Man is entirely subservient to the intangible force which comes with a thunderstorm, and he is just as helpless in the presence of the intangible force of electricity—nay, he does not even know what electricity is, where it comes from, or what is its purpose!

Nor is this by any means the end of man's ignorance in connection with things unseen and intangible. He does not understand the intangible force (and intelligence) wrapped up in the soil of the earth—*the force which provides him with every morsel of food he eats, every article of clothing he wears, every dollar he carries in his pockets.*

November 30

Man, with all of his boasted culture and education, understands little or nothing of the greatest of all the intangibles—*thought*. He knows but little concerning the physical brain, and its vast network of intricate machinery through which the power of thought is translated into its material equivalent, but he is now entering an age which shall yield enlightenment on the subject. Already men of science have uncovered enough knowledge to know that the central switchboard of the human brain, the number of lines which connect the brain cells one with another, equal the figure one, followed by fifteen million ciphers.

It is inconceivable that such a network of intricate machinery should be in existence for the sole purpose of carrying on the physical functions incidental to growth and maintenance of the physical body. Is it not likely that the same system which gives billions of brain cells the media for communication one with another provides also the means of communication with other intangible forces?

DECEMBER

The Thirteenth Step Toward Riches

THE SIXTH SENSE

AND

HOW TO OUTWIT THE SIX GHOSTS OF FEAR

December 1

The "thirteenth" principle is known as the sixth sense, through which Infinite Intelligence may, and will, communicate voluntarily without any effort from, or demands by, the individual. This principle is the apex of the philosophy. It can be assimilated, understood, and applied only by first mastering the other twelve principles.

The sixth sense is that portion of the subconscious mind which has been referred to as the Creative Imagination. It has also been referred to as the "receiving set" through which ideas, plans, and thoughts flash into the mind. The "flashes" are sometimes called "hunches" or "inspirations."

December 2

The sixth sense defies description! It cannot be described to a person who has not mastered the other principles of this philosophy, because such a person has no knowledge and no experience with which the sixth sense may be compared.

Understanding of the sixth sense comes only by meditation through mind development *from within*. The sixth sense probably is the medium of contact between the finite mind of man and Infinite Intelligence, and for this reason *it is a mixture of both the mental and the spiritual*. It is believed to be the point at which the mind of man contacts the Universal Mind.

December 3

Through the aid of the sixth sense, you will be warned of impending dangers in time to avoid them and notified of opportunities in time to embrace them. There comes to your aid, and to do your bidding, with the development of the sixth sense, a "guardian angel" who will open to you at all times the door to the Temple of Wisdom.

December 4

Nature *never deviates from her established laws*. Some of her laws are so incomprehensible that they produce what appear to be "miracles." The sixth sense comes as near to being a miracle as anything I have ever experienced, and it appears so, only because I do not understand the method by which this principle is operated.

There is a power, or a First Cause, or an Intelligence, which permeates every atom of matter and embraces every unit of energy perceptible to man—that this Infinite Intelligence converts acorns into oak trees, causes water to flow downhill in response to the law of gravity, follows night with day, and winter with summer, each maintaining its proper place and relationship to the other. This Intelligence may, through the principles of this philosophy, be induced to aid in transmuting desires into concrete or material form. The author has this knowledge, because he has experimented with it—and has experienced it.

December 5

Somewhere in the cell structure of the brain is located an organ which receives vibrations of thought ordinarily called "hunches." So far, science has not discovered where this organ of the sixth sense is located, but this is not important. The fact remains that human beings do receive accurate knowledge through sources other than the physical senses. Such knowledge, generally, is received when the mind is under the influence of extraordinary stimulation. Any emergency which arouses the emotions and causes the heart to beat more rapidly than normal may, and generally does, bring the sixth sense into action. Anyone who has experienced a near accident while driving knows that on such occasions the sixth sense often comes to one's rescue and aids, by split seconds, in avoiding the accident.

December 6

The sixth sense is not something that one can take off and put on at will. Ability to use this great power comes slowly through application of the other principles outlined in this book. Seldom does any individual come into workable knowledge of the sixth sense before the age of forty. More often the knowledge is not available until one is well past fifty, and this, for the reason that the spiritual forces with which the sixth sense is so closely related, does not mature and become usable except through years of meditation, self-examination, and serious thought.

No matter who you are, or what may have been your purpose in reading this book, you can profit by it without understanding this principle. This is especially true if your major purpose is that of accumulation of money or other material things.

December 7

The starting point of all achievement is desire. The finishing point is that brand of knowledge which leads to understanding—understanding of self, understanding of others, understanding of the laws of Nature, recognition and understanding of happiness.

This sort of understanding comes in its fullness only through familiarity with and use of the principle of the sixth sense; hence that principle had to be included as a part of this philosophy for the benefit of those who demand more than money.

December 8

There are six fears which are the cause of all discouragement, timidity, procrastination, indifference, indecision, and the lack of ambition, self-reliance, initiative, self-control, and enthusiasm. There are six basic fears, with some combination of which every human suffers at one time or another. Most people are fortunate if they do not suffer from the entire six. Named in the order of their most common appearance, they are:

The fear of Poverty
The fear of Criticism
The fear of Ill Health
The fear of Loss of Love of someone
The fear of Old Age
The fear of Death

Search yourself carefully as you study these six enemies, as they may exist only in your subconscious mind, where their presence will be hard to detect.

Remember, as you analyze the "Six Ghosts of Fear," that they are nothing but ghosts because they exist only in one's mind. Remember, also, that ghosts—creations of uncontrolled imagination—have caused most of the damage people have done to their own minds; therefore ghosts can be as dangerous as if they lived and walked on the earth in physical bodies.

December 9

Before you can put any portion of this philosophy into successful use, your mind must be prepared to receive it. The preparation is not difficult. It begins with study, analysis, and understanding of three enemies which you shall have to clear out.

These are indecision, doubt, and fear!

The sixth sense will never function while these three negatives, or any of them remain in your mind. The members of this unholy trio are closely related; where one is found, the other two are close at hand.

Indecision is the seedling of fear! Remember this as you read. Indecision crystallizes into doubt; the two blend and become fear! The "blending" process often is slow. This is one reason why these three enemies are so dangerous. They germinate and grow *without their presence being observed.*

December 10

Before we can master an enemy, we must know its name, its habits, and its place of abode. As you read, analyze yourself carefully, and determine which, if any, of the six common fears (*listed on December 8*) have attached themselves to you.

Do not be deceived by the habits of these subtle enemies. Sometimes they remain hidden in the subconscious mind, where they are difficult to locate and still more difficult to eliminate.

December 11

The prevalence of these fears, as a curse to the world, runs in cycles. For almost six years, while the Depression was on, we floundered in the cycle of fear of Poverty. During the world war, we were in the cycle of fear of Death. Just following the war, we were in the cycle of fear of Ill Health, as evidenced by the epidemic of disease which spread itself all over the world.

Fears are nothing more than states of mind. One's state of mind is subject to control and direction. Physicians, as everyone knows, are less subject to attack by disease than ordinary laymen, for the reason that physicians do not fear disease. Physicians, without fear or hesitation, have been known to physically contact hundreds of people, daily, who were suffering from such contagious diseases as small-pox, without becoming infected. Their immunity against the disease consisted largely, if not solely, in their absolute lack of fear.

December 12

Man can create nothing of which he does not first conceive in the form of an impulse of thought. Following this statement comes another of still greater importance, namely man's thought impulses begin immediately to translate themselves into their physical equivalent, whether those thoughts are voluntary or involuntary. Thought impulses which are picked up through the ether by mere chance (thoughts which have been released by other minds) may determine one's financial, business, professional, or social destiny just as surely as do the thought impulses which one creates by intent and design.

December 13

We are here laying the foundation for the presentation of a fact of great importance to the person who does not understand why some people appear to be "lucky" while others of equal or greater ability, training, experience, and brain capacity seem destined to ride with misfortune. This fact may be explained by the statement that *every human being has the ability to completely control his own mind,* and with this control, obviously, every person may open his mind to the tramp thought impulses which are being released by other brains, or close the doors tightly and admit only thought impulses of his own choice.

December 14

Nature has endowed man with absolute control over but one thing, and that is thought. This fact, coupled with the additional fact that everything which man creates begins in the form of a thought, leads one very near to the principle by which fear may be mastered.

If it is true that all thought has a tendency to clothe itself in its physical equivalent (and this is true beyond any reasonable room for doubt), it is equally true that thought impulses of fear and poverty cannot be translated into terms of courage and financial gain.

The people of America began to think of poverty following the Wall Street crash of 1929. Slowly but surely that mass thought was crystallized into its physical equivalent, which was known as a "depression." This had to happen; it is in conformity with the laws of Nature.

December 15

There can be no compromise between poverty and riches! The two roads that lead to poverty and riches travel in opposite directions. If you want riches, you must refuse to accept any circumstance that leads toward poverty. (The word *riches* is here used in its broadest sense, meaning financial, spiritual, mental, and material estates.) The starting point of the path that leads to riches is desire.

Here, then, is the place to give yourself a challenge which will definitely determine how much of this philosophy you have absorbed. Here is the point at which you can turn prophet and foretell, accurately, what the future holds in store for you. If you are willing to accept poverty, you may as well make up your mind to receive poverty. This is one decision you cannot avoid.

December 16

If you demand riches, determine what form and how much will be required to satisfy you. You know the road that leads to riches. You have been given a road map which, if followed, will keep you on that road. If you neglect to make the start, or stop before you arrive, no one will be to blame but you. This responsibility is yours. No alibi will save you from accepting the responsibility if you now fail or refuse to demand riches of Life, because the acceptance calls for but one thing—incidentally, the only thing you can control—and that is a state of mind. A state of mind is something that one assumes. It cannot be purchased; it must be created.

December 17

The Ghost of the Fear of Poverty, which seized the minds of millions of people in 1929, was so real that it caused the worst business depression this country has ever known.

Fear of poverty is a state of mind, nothing else! But it is sufficient to destroy one's chances of achievement in any undertaking, a truth which became painfully evident during the Depression.

This fear paralyzes the faculty of reason, destroys the faculty of imagination, kills off self-reliance, undermines enthusiasm, discourages initiative, leads to uncertainty of purpose, encourages procrastination, wipes out enthusiasm, and makes self-control an impossibility. It takes the charm from one's personality, destroys the possibility of accurate thinking, diverts concentration of effort; it masters persistence, turns the willpower into nothingness, destroys ambition, beclouds the memory, and invites failure in every conceivable form; it kills love and assassinates the finer emotions of the heart, discourages friendship and invites disaster in a hundred forms, leads to sleeplessness, misery, and unhappiness—and all this despite the obvious truth that we live in a world of overabundance of everything the heart could desire, with nothing standing between us and our desires, excepting lack of a definite purpose.

December 18

The Fear of Poverty is, without doubt, the most destructive of the six basic fears. It has been placed at the head of the list, because it is the most difficult to master. Considerable courage is required to state the truth about the origin of this fear and still greater courage to accept the truth after it has been stated. The fear of poverty grew out of man's inherited tendency to prey upon his fellow man economically. Nearly all animals lower than man are motivated by instinct, but their capacity to "think" is limited; therefore, they prey upon one another physically. Man, with his superior sense of intuition, with the capacity to think and to reason, does not eat his fellow man bodily; he gets more satisfaction out of "eating" him financially. Man is so avaricious that every conceivable law has been passed to safeguard him from his fellow man.

Nothing brings man so much suffering and humility as poverty! Only those who have experienced poverty understand the full meaning of this.

December 19

SYMPTOMS OF THE FEAR OF POVERTY

Indifference: lack of ambition; willingness to tolerate poverty; mental and physical laziness; lack of initiative, imagination, enthusiasm, and self-control.

Indecision: permitting others to do one's thinking; staying "on the fence."

Doubt: alibis and excuses to cover up, explain away, or apologize for one's failures, sometimes expressed in the form of envy of those who are successful or of criticism of them.

Worry: finding fault with others, spending beyond one's income, neglect of personal appearance, scowling and frowning; nervousness, lack of poise, self-consciousness, and lack of self-reliance.

Over-caution: looking for the negative side of every circumstance, thinking of possible failure instead of the means of succeeding. Knowing all roads to disaster but never planning to avoid failure. Waiting for "the right time" to put ideas and plans into action until the waiting becomes permanent.

Procrastination: putting off until tomorrow that which should have been done last year. Refusal to accept responsibility when it can be avoided. Willingness to compromise rather than put up a stiff fight. Bargaining with Life for a penny, instead of demanding prosperity, contentment, and happiness. Association with those who accept poverty instead of seeking the company of those who demand and receive riches.

December 20

The Fear of Criticism takes on many forms, the majority of which are petty and trivial.

The fear of criticism robs man of his initiative, destroys his power of imagination, limits his individuality, takes away his self-reliance, and does him damage in a hundred other ways. Parents often do their children irreparable injury by criticizing them.

Criticism is the one form of service of which everyone has too much. Everyone has a stock of it which is handed out, gratis, whether called for or not. One's nearest relatives often are the worst offenders. It should be recognized as a crime (in reality it is a crime of the worst nature) for any parent to build inferiority complexes in the mind of a child through unnecessary criticism.

Employers who understand human nature get the best there is in men, not by criticism but by constructive suggestion. Parents may accomplish the same results with their children. Criticism will plant fear in the human heart or resentment, but it will not build love or affection.

This fear is almost as universal as the fear of poverty, and its effects are just as fatal to personal achievement, mainly because this fear destroys initiative and discourages the use of imagination.

December 21

SYMPTOMS OF THE FEAR OF CRITICISM

Self-consciousness: generally expressed through nervousness, timidity in conversation and in meeting strangers, awkward movement of the hands and limbs, shifting of the eyes.

Lack of poise: expressed through lack of voice control, nervousness in the presence of others, poor posture of body, poor memory.

Personality: lacking firmness of decision, personal charm, and ability to express opinions definitely. Sidestepping issues instead of meeting them squarely. Agreeing with others without careful examination of their opinions.

Inferiority complex: expressing self-approval by word of mouth and by actions as a means of covering up a feeling of inferiority. Using "big words" to impress. Imitating others in dress, speech, and manners. Boasting of imaginary achievements.

Extravagance: trying to "keep up with the Joneses," spending beyond one's income.

Lack of initiative: failure to embrace opportunities,

fear to express opinions, lack of confidence in one's own ideas, giving evasive answers, hesitant manner, deceit in words and deeds.

Lack of ambition: mental and physical laziness, slowness in reaching decisions, easily influenced by others, criticizing others behind their backs, accepting defeat without protest, quitting an undertaking when opposed by others, suspicious of other people without cause, lacking in tactfulness of manner and speech, unwillingness to accept the blame for mistakes.

December 22

Fear of Ill Health may be traced to both physical and social heredity. It is closely associated, as to its origin, with the causes of fear of Old Age and the fear of Death, because it leads one closely to the border of "terrible worlds" of which man knows not but concerning which he has been taught some discomforting stories.

There is overwhelming evidence that disease sometimes begins in the form of negative thought impulse. Such an impulse may be passed from one mind to another by suggestion or created by an individual in his own mind. It has been shown most convincingly that the fear of disease, even where there is not the slightest cause for fear, often produces the physical symptoms of the disease feared.

In the main, man fears ill health because of the terrible pictures which have been planted in his mind of what may happen if death should overtake him. He also fears it because of the economic toll which it may claim.

December 23

SYMPTOMS OF THE FEAR OF ILL HEALTH

Auto-suggestion: negative use of self-suggestion by looking for, and expecting to find, the symptoms of all kinds of disease. "Enjoying" imaginary illness as if real. Trying all "fads" and "isms" recommended as having therapeutic value. Talking of operations, accidents, and other forms of illness. Experimenting with diets and physical exercises without professional guidance.

Hypochondria: talking of illness, concentrating upon disease, and expecting its appearance until a nervous break occurs. (Nothing that comes in bottles can cure this condition. It is brought on by negative thinking, and nothing but positive thought can effect a cure.)

Exercise: fear of ill health often interferes with proper physical exercise and results in overweight by causing one to avoid outdoor life.

Susceptibility: fear of ill health breaks down Nature's body resistance and creates a favorable condition for any form of disease one may contact.

Self-coddling: making a bid for sympathy using imaginary illness. (People often resort to this trick to avoid work.) Feigning illness to cover laziness or use as an alibi for lack of ambition.

Intemperance: using alcohol or narcotics to destroy pains instead of eliminating their cause. Reading about illness and worrying over the possibility of being stricken by it.

December 24

The source of the Fear of Loss of Love needs but little description, because it obviously grew out of man's polygamous habit of stealing his fellow man's mate and his habit of taking liberties with her whenever he could.

Jealousy and other similar forms of dementia prae-cox grow out of man's inherited fear of the loss of love of someone. This fear is the most painful of all the six basic fears. It probably plays more havoc with the body and mind than any of the other basic fears, as it often leads to permanent insanity.

December 25

SYMPTOMS OF THE FEAR OF LOSS OF LOVE

Jealousy: being suspicious of friends and loved ones without any reasonable evidence or sufficient grounds. (Jealousy is a form of dementia praecox which sometimes becomes violent without the slightest cause.) The habit of accusing wife or husband of infidelity without grounds. General suspicion of everyone, absolute faith in no one.

Faultfinding: finding fault with friends, relatives, business associates, and loved ones upon the slightest provocation or without any cause whatsoever.

Gambling: gambling, stealing, cheating, and otherwise taking hazardous chances to provide money for loved ones, with the belief that love can be bought. Spending beyond one's means, or incurring debts, to provide gifts for loved ones, with the object of making a favorable showing. Insomnia, nervousness, lack of persistence, weakness of will, lack of self-control, lack of self-reliance, bad temper.

December 26

The Fear of Old Age grows out of two sources. First, the thought that old age may bring with it poverty.

Secondly, and by far the most common source of origin, from false and cruel teachings of the past, which have been too well mixed with "fire and brimstone," and other bogies cunningly designed to enslave man through fear.

The possibility of ill health, which is more common as people grow older, is also a contributing cause of this common fear of old age.

Another contributing cause of the fear of old age is the possibility of loss of freedom and independence, as old age may bring with it the loss of both physical and economic freedom.

December 27

SYMPTOMS OF THE FEAR OF OLD AGE

The tendency to slow down and develop an inferiority complex at the age of mental maturity, around the age of forty, falsely believing oneself to be "slipping" because of age. (The truth is that man's most useful years, mentally and spiritually, are those between forty and sixty.)

The habit of speaking apologetically of one's self as "being old" merely because one has reached the age of forty or fifty, instead of reversing the rule and expressing gratitude for having reached the age of wisdom and understanding.

The habit of killing off initiative, imagination, and self-reliance by falsely believing one's self too old to exercise these qualities. The habit of the man or woman of forty dressing with the aim of trying to appear much younger and affecting mannerisms of youth, thereby inspiring ridicule by both friends and strangers.

December 28

To some the Fear of Death is the cruelest of all the basic fears. The reason is obvious: The terrible pangs of fear associated with the thought of death, in the majority of cases, may be charged directly to religious fanaticism. So-called "heathens" are less afraid of death than the more "civilized." For hundreds of millions of years man has been asking the still-unanswered questions "whence" and "whither." Where did I come from, and where am I going? Insane asylums are filled with men and women who have gone mad because of the fear of death.

This fear is useless. Death will come, no matter what anyone may think about it. Accept it as a necessity, and pass the thought out of your mind. It must be a necessity, or it would not come to all. Perhaps it is not as bad as it has been pictured.

December 29

SYMPTOMS OF THE FEAR OF DEATH

The habit of thinking about dying instead of making the most of life is due, generally, to lack of purpose or lack of a suitable occupation. This fear is more prevalent among the aged, but sometimes the more youthful are victims of it. The greatest of all remedies for the fear of death is a burning desire for achievement, backed by useful service to others. A busy person seldom has time to think about dying. He finds life too thrilling to worry about death. Sometimes the Fear of Death is closely associated with the Fear of Poverty, where one's death would leave loved ones poverty stricken. In other cases, the fear of death is caused by illness and the consequent breaking down of physical body resistance. The commonest causes of the fear of death are: ill health, poverty, lack of appropriate occupation, disappointment over love, insanity, religious fanaticism.

December 30

Worry is a state of mind based upon fear. It works slowly but persistently. It is insidious and subtle. Step by step it "digs itself in" until it paralyzes one's reasoning faculty and destroys self-confidence and initiative. Worry is a form of sustained fear caused by indecision; therefore it is a state of mind which can be controlled.

An unsettled mind is helpless. Indecision makes an unsettled mind. Most individuals lack the willpower to reach decisions promptly and to stand by them after they have been made, even during normal business conditions. During periods of economic unrest (such as the world recently experienced), the individual is handicapped, not alone by his inherent nature to be slow at reaching decisions but he is influenced by the indecision of others around him who have created a state of "mass indecision."

December 31

L ife is a checkerboard, and the player opposite you is time. If you hesitate before moving, or neglect to move promptly, your men will be wiped off the board by time. You are playing against a partner who will not tolerate indecision!"

Previously you may have had a logical excuse for not having forced Life to come through with whatever you asked, but that alibi is now obsolete, because you are in possession of the Master Key that unlocks the door to Life's bountiful riches.

The Master Key is intangible, but it is powerful! It is the privilege of creating, *in your own mind,* a burning desire for a definite form of riches. There is no penalty for the use of the Key, but there is a price you must pay if you do not use it. The price is failure. There is a reward of stupendous proportions if you put the Key to use. It is the satisfaction that comes to all who *conquer self and force Life to pay whatever is asked.*

The reward is worthy of your effort. Will you make the start and be convinced?

Notes

Notes

Notes

Notes

About the Author

Napoleon Hill was born in 1883, in Wise County, Virginia. He worked as a secretary, a "mountain reporter" for a local newspaper, and the manager of a coal mine and a lumberyard, and attended law school, before he began working as a journalist for *Bob Taylor's Magazine*—a job that led to his meeting steel magnate Andrew Carnegie, which changed the course of his life. Carnegie believed success could be distilled into principles that any person could follow and urged Hill to interview the greatest industrialists of the era in order to discover these principles. Hill took on the challenge, which lasted twenty years and formed the building block for *Think and Grow Rich*. This wealth-building classic and all-time bestseller of its kind has sold more than 15 million copies worldwide. Hill devoted the remainder of his life to discovering and refining the principles of success. After a long and rich career as an author, magazine publisher, lecturer, and consultant to business leaders, the motivational pioneer died in 1970, in South Carolina.

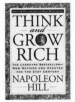

The Master-Key to Riches by Napoleon Hill
Here is the actual handbook that Napoleon Hill
provided to certified teachers of his ideas—a
master class from the greatest motivational
writer of all time, revised and updated for the
twenty-first century.   ISBN 978-1-58542-709-3
*On sale now • $10.00   Also available from Penguin
Audio   ISBN 978-0-14-314461-8 • $19.95*

How to Prosper in Hard Times by Napoleon Hill,
James Allen, Joseph Murphy, and others
This is the ultimate prosperity survival guide for
tough times, featuring ageless wisdom and essential
insights from the greatest motivational writers ever.
ISBN 978-1-58542-755-0   *On sale now • $12.95*
Also available from Penguin Audio
ISBN 978-0-14-314482-3 • $29.95

The Think and Grow Rich Workbook
by Napoleon Hill
For the millions of people who have read and loved
Think and Grow Rich, here—for the first time—is a
workbook and companion to the classic bestseller.
ISBN 978-1-58542-711-6   *On sale now • $18.95*

Think and Grow Rich Every Day by Napoleon Hill
Using the most potent writings from Hill's books,
Think and Grow Rich and *The Law of Success,*
these daily readings will help to turn doubt into
confidence, fear into strength, and failure into
triumph.   ISBN 978-1-58542-811-3
On sale now • $14.95/$18.95 Canada

The Magic Ladder to Success by Napoleon Hill
This compact powerful primer in success-building
is Napoleon Hill's distillation of his lifetime of
learning, now revised and updated for the twenty-
first century.   ISBN 978-1-58542-710-9
On sale now • $10.00

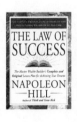

The Law of Success by Napoleon Hill
Here is Napoleon Hill's first pioneering work,
featuring the fullest exploration of his formula for
achievement, in fifteen remarkable steps—newly
redesigned and reset.   ISBN 978-1-58542-689-8
On sale now • $16.95
Also available from Penguin Audio
ISBN 978-0-14-314419-9 • $29.95

Your Magic Power to Be Rich! by Napoleon Hill
The ultimate Napoleon Hill resource, featuring
updated editions of the master motivator's greatest
books: *Think and Grow Rich, The Magic Ladder to
Success, and The Master-Key to Riches.*
ISBN 978-1-58542-555-6   *On sale now • $16.95*

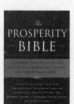

The Prosperity Bible
Featuring beloved classics by Napoleon Hill,
Benjamin Franklin, James Allen, Wallace D.
Wattles, Ernest Holmes, Florence Scovel Shinn,
and many other. This beautiful and durable boxed
volume collects the greatest success writing ever for
a lifetime resource in self-empowerment.
ISBN 978-1-58542-614-0   *On sale now • $35.00*

Tarcher Success Classics

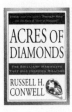

Acres of Diamonds by Russell H. Conwell
The stirring manifesto shows how to discover
everything you need to succeed—where you least
expect if. Features the rare bonus works *The Story of
Acres of Diamonds* and *Praying for Money*.
ISBN 978-1-58542-690-4   *On sale now • $10.00*

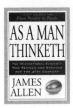

As a Man Thinketh by James Allen
A revised and updated edition of one of the world's
best-selling and most widely loved inspirational
works—also features, as a special bonus, an updated
edition of the author's first book, *From Poverty to
Power.*   ISBN 978-1-58542-638-6
On sale now • $10.00

The Game of Life and How to Play It
by Florence Scovel Shinn
Here is one of the most famous motivational works of the twentieth century, *The Game of Life and How to Play It*, grouped together with three other short books by Florence Scovel Shinn, for an all-in-one definitive volume. ISBN 978-1-58542-745-1
On sale now • $10.00

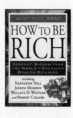

How to Be Rich by Napoleon Hill, Joseph Murphy, Ph.D., D.D., Wallace D. Wattles, Robert Collier
The accumulated wisdom of the most celebrated motivational writers of all time is distilled into one brief playbook for unlocking the prosperity-power of your mind. ISBN 978-1-58542-821-2
On sale now • $25.95

In Tune with the Infinite by Ralph Waldo Trine
One of the most powerful self-improvement books ever written, this life-changing classic shows how thoughts shape your destiny.
ISBN 978-1-58542-663-8 *On sale now • $10.00*

The Master Key System by Charles F. Haanel
The all-time classic shows how to use the "Law of
Attraction" in your life.   ISBN 978-1-58542-627-0
On sale now • $10.00

A Message to Garcia by Elbert Hubbard
This tale of a soldier's self-reliance during the
Spanish-American War is one of history's greatest
motivational lessons, now collected with Elbert
Hubbard's most treasured inspirational essays.
ISBN 978-1-58542-691-1   *On sale now • $10.00*

Mind Is the Master by James Allen
The classic books of the motivational visionary,
collected for the first time in a single volume.
ISBN 978-1-58542-769-7   *On sale now • $19.95*

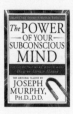

Power of Your Subconscious Mind
by Joseph Murphy, Ph.D., D.D.
Here is the complete, original text of the millions-
selling self-help guide that reveals your invisible
power to attain any goal—paired with a compelling
bonus work, *How to Attract Money.*
ISBN 978-1-58542-768-0   *On sale now • $10.00*

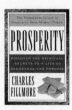

Prosperity by Charles Fillmore
The lessons of Scripture reveal the hidden keys to
prosperity—discover how to use them to create
abundance and purpose in your life.
ISBN 978-1-58542-674-4   *On sale now • $10.00*

Public Speaking for Success by Dale Carnegie
The definitive edition of Dale Carnegie's public-
speaking bible—now revised and updated for the
twenty-first century.   ISBN 978-1-58542-492-4
On sale now • $12.95

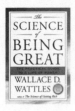

The Science of Being Great by Wallace D. Wattles
Discover the rules of real power and personal
achievement in this extraordinary companion to
The Science of Getting Rich.   ISBN 978-1-58542-628-7
On sale now • $10.00
Also available from Penguin Audio
ISBN 978-0-14-314284-3 • $19.95

The Science of Getting Rich by Wallace D. Wattles
The time-tested mental program to a life of
wealth—also features the rare bonus work "How to
Get What You Want."   ISBN 978-1-58542-601-0
On sale now • $10.00
Also available from Penguin Audio
ISBN 978-0-14-314269-9 • $19.95

The Secret of the Ages by Robert Collier
How to attain the life you want—by tapping the
incredible visualizing faculties of your mind.
ISBN 978-1-58542-629-4   *On sale now • $10.00*
Also available from Penguin Audio
ISBN 978-0-14-314340-6 • $29.95